SIMON PEARCE

Design for Living

GLENN SUOKKO

With a foreword by Simon Pearce and a contribution by Margaret Downes

London · Milan · New York · Paris

FOREWORD

SIMON PEARCE

The two topics that interest most people about my career are: Why glass? How did you get started?

Why glass? I have been interested in design since childhood. I was fortunate to grow up with parents who were passionate about design—whether it was the wrought-iron gates, baskets, and ceramics of Ireland, antique English and Irish wooden furniture, or the latest Scandinavian table accessories and furnishings of the time.

When I was a teenager, I was drawn to classic simple forms and functional designs, and, personally, form and function were critically intertwined. If an object didn't work properly, no matter how beautiful it was I wouldn't consider it to be good design. The Georgian period exemplifies my aesthetic best—the design is elegant and practical, whether it is architecture, furniture, flatware, or glass. So when I started looking closely at the glass from this period, I realized my goal was to eventually produce something of such exquisite quality. Over the years, my ideas have evolved but I still think much of what we at Simon Pearce make today has the same qualities. Glass is a wonderful medium to design and work with, as the possibilities are virtually limitless. The most important thing I learned is to be careful not to get carried away and make something too ornate or unnecessarily complicated. I still find that for me, the simpler it is, the more beautiful it is.

How I got started? Thanks to my friend and author Glenn Suokko, I'm confident you will find the answers within the pages of this book. His words as well as his spectacular photography tell the entire story better than I ever could.

One of the most important and special parts of my life designing and making glass has been the involvement of my family, especially my wife, Pia. Since our start in Ireland, she has been essential to the success of every aspect of Simon Pearce. She and our four boys have never been shy about telling me what they think about our latest creations. I could not have done it without her.

OPPOSITE
Simon designed the
Essex bowl in 2015.

THE EARLY DAYS IN IRELAND

MARGARET DOWNES

The Pearce family home in Shanagarry, County Cork, Ireland, was always full of interesting people—poets, painters, designers, writers, theater people, and businesspeople—whom my family and I loved to visit.

Simon, his older brother, Stephen, and his younger sister, Sarah, were afforded an idyllic and free lifestyle in a splendid Georgian house in the beautiful Cork countryside of southeastern Ireland. Simon's mother, Lucy, a high academic achiever, was one of the first female university professors in Britain, with a special interest in biology and human health. Simon's father, Philip, a gentle, shy man, was inherently interested in design. Philip's artistic, creative side led him to establish Shanagarry Pottery and with great success it became Ireland's leading hand-thrown pottery. And from this solid base the young Simon, generally disinterested in academic achievement, persuaded his parents to allow him to leave boarding school at sixteen to develop his deep appreciation and respect for design. It was at this stage of Simon's life that I met him. Over the many years that followed, we have been blessed with an enduring friendship that has survived time and distance apart. Our friendship was tested on a number of occasions by pranks, especially when, right before the ceremony and his marriage to Pia McDonnell, he threw me into the swimming pool at her parents' house.

Simon's early ambition was to become a potter, so he spent time training under his father and became an expert potter, a talent he retains to this day. However, as his brother, Stephen, was destined to take over and develop their father's Shanagarry Pottery, Simon decided to shift from pottery making to hand-blown glass. Patrick Scott, a

OPPOSITE
Kilmahon House,
the Pearce family
home in Shanagarry,
Ireland, 1960s.

frequent visitor to the Pearce house and one of Ireland's leading modern painters, had a superb collection of antique Irish hand-blown glass, and it inspired Simon to make the transition to create glass. After the death of his friend and godfather, Patrick Scott, Simon inherited his glass collection. As with everything he undertakes, Simon sought perfection, which led him to study glassblowing with master craftsmen in many countries, winding up at the world-famous Orrefors glass factory in Sweden. Having returned to Ireland in the early 1970s, the always-ambitious Simon set up his own hand-blown glassmaking facility at Bennettsbridge in County Kilkenny.

In the 1960s, the state-owned Kilkenny Design Workshops had been established to develop and promote quality design in Ireland. Simon's well-designed hand-blown glass was an integral part of the design movement in Ireland. His beautifully designed glass in simple forms caught the eye of those who appreciated quality products, and his glass was an immediate success. To this day, his original Irish hand-blown wine glasses, rummers, and jugs are greatly admired and treasured.

Establishing his glass business in the 1970s was a great challenge for Simon. Design appreciation was not seriously valued in Ireland at the time and the concept of providing funds to a young man to establish a new glass factory was not high on the list of a bank manager's priorities—and certainly not the notion of an ideal client. Simon and I (a young partner in PricewaterhouseCoopers at the time) made a number of visits to various banks in Cork before securing funds to build his new glass facility and to install his furnaces. At the same time, he designed and developed a splendid new home, amalgamating and converting two old cottages, where he and his young bride, Pia, spent the first few years of their married life.

In 1980, Ireland sadly lost this innovative and creative master craftsman to Vermont in the United States, where he established his hugely successful American hand-blown glass business, Simon Pearce.

OPPOSITE
Simon (foreground) in his first glass workshop in Bennettsbridge, Ireland, 1970s.

INTRODUCTION

Most creative individuals develop design skills in art schools, while others learn from experience. Simon Pearce was fortunate to be raised in an environment where he saw beautifully crafted functional objects created at his family's Shanagarry Pottery in rural Ireland on a daily basis. His early life experiences in the countryside and working in his father's pottery formed his creative spirit. Simon was first a potter, but his ultimate talent as a glass designer comes from his experience as a glassblower. He learned how to make glass before designing glassware. Simon was never interested in creating one-of-a-kind art pieces in glass; his intention early on was to design and make glassware to use every day at the table, in the home—in essence, design for living.

Although known primarily for his extensive lines of functional handmade glassware, Simon also makes pottery and has designed dinnerware as well as flatware and lighting to provide a complete range of home accessories. The simple yet sophisticated life that Simon first knew in Ireland and the way of living that he and his wife, Pia, created in Vermont, inform Simon's product designs, and these qualities have inspired a Simon Pearce lifestyle.

I first learned of Simon Pearce in the late 1980s when I was a design student attending graduate school and happened upon a magazine article about the Vermont-based glassblower. In contrast to the erudite design world I was eager to embrace, Simon's approach to design and making utilitarian objects based on the old-fashioned craft of glassblowing was very different and refreshing. Many years later I met Pia and Simon in Vermont and collaborated with them on *A Way of Living*, a book that is an expression of their lifestyle.

Simon Pearce: Design for Living furthers their story by focusing on Simon's early influences in Ireland, his designs for glass, his collection of pottery, and the seminal potters, craftsmen, and artists who inspire him.

Through the many interviews and conversations I have had with Simon over the years that led to the creation of this book, I became aware of the significance of particular places, the importance of certain people, and the lineage of philosophies that had an ultimate effect on Simon's glass. Those influences are the foundation of this story.

Since he began making glass in the early 1970s, Simon has designed a lot of objects. However, in the bustle of running a business he did not always keep detailed records, so the dating of the illustrated works is approximate. Throughout this book, a wide range of glass from the last four decades has been selected by Simon and me to exemplify his most notable work. Many designs originated in Ireland, carried over to Vermont, and remain in production and some have been retired to make room for new pieces. Today, under Simon's guidance, a new generation of designers creates glass and pottery in the spirit of his designs. Examples of their work are presented in the chapter "Selected Designs."

For Simon, he is honored that so many people turn to his glass and pottery to use in their homes, especially knowing the impact that being surrounded by beautiful handmade wares had on him during his childhood. There are countless untold stories that result as tables are set, candleholders are lit, bowls are passed, plates are served, glasses are raised, and conversations begin. This is when design comes to life.

OPPOSITE
A table set with Simon's luminous glass.

FROM IRELAND TO VERMONT
A LIFE MAKING GLASS

Simon Pearce's early life on the southeastern coast of Ireland made a deep and everlasting impression on his creative spirit. The formative experiences he had there would later become the anchor of his work as a designer and glassmaker in Vermont. With a penchant for Georgian-period glass, hand blown in the eighteenth and nineteenth centuries, and a strong sense of design, Simon began in the early 1970s to redefine the anachronistic craft of glassblowing. His goal was not only to create glass that was both functional and beautiful, but also to build a business making and selling his creations.

Inspired by older forms and styles, Simon's early glass designs that he produced as a young man in Ireland remained fixed in his design memory. After he moved to rural Vermont, his intentions matured and his innovative glassmaking techniques allowed him to explore the craft further, and with technological advances he developed his own refined modern aesthetic. Today, in an era when virtually all glass is manufactured and

finished by machines, and scale and speed are a necessity for commercial viability, Simon Pearce—choosing to make each piece of glass by hand, one at a time—remains a leader in the field.

Utility is the essential objective in Simon's glassware—most of his designs are for domestic use. Individuality is a prominent feature in his glass. Simon was never interested in crafting one-of-a-kind pieces as an artisan might; however, the process of blowing and making glass by hand ensures that no two pieces of any one design are exactly alike. Placed side by side, his wine glasses may show slight differences in the height, shape, or the width of the drinking bowl. More distinct differences are visible in his decorative Vermont Evergreens, a design for glass trees that is truly unique each and every time. Subtle individuality is the hallmark of Simon Pearce glassware—customers and collectors are drawn to the unique character and qualities it possesses.

Simon's quest to celebrate "the humanness" in his glass is in part his reaction to the impersonal feeling of mass-produced objects, in which all surfaces, shapes, and lines are absolutely perfect and always the same. He finds beauty in the imperfect, a concept that comes out of two distinct cultures: the English and Irish design heritages strongly rooted in the Georgian era and the intangible spirit of ancient utilitarian pottery. Significant in the foundation of both of these "design" cultures is that the objects are handmade. There are inevitable imperfections and it is precisely these nuances that are appreciated by many as beautiful, even special, because they are made by people and not machines.

Revered for its design and quality, Simon Pearce glass is known and respected all over the world. Many people can look at a wine glass and say, "That is a Simon Pearce glass," or, "That is definitely not Simon Pearce!" What is not widely recognized is why Simon Pearce glass can be identified so readily. The intangibles live in the objects themselves, but perhaps most invisibly and deeply in Simon's personal story.

The rugged shore of Ballycotton Bay on the southeastern coast of Ireland, where Simon spent his youth.

OPPOSITE
Simon created the Large bowl in Ireland and carried the design over to production in Vermont, where it was further developed and renamed the Shelburne bowl, shown here set against the dramatic Ballycotton Bay.

SHAPED BY COUNTRY LIFE
IN IRELAND

There isn't any one particular event that formed my interests in design or glass while I lived in Ireland, but it was the place—all of it, collectively—that had an affect on me. Shanagarry, where I spent the most time, was a beautiful place and life was very simple back then. I always felt that the outdoors, the land, sea, and sky, and the people, the food—really, all of it together—made the difference.

—SIMON PEARCE

In the early 1940s, Simon's father, Philip Pearce, a typographer and printer working in his father's printing business in London, sought a simpler and more healthy life in the country, and he received a modest inheritance that provided him with the means to realize his aspiration. By train, by bus, on bicycle, and on foot, Philip explored Ireland and eventually found his dream in Shanagarry, a small fishing and farming village on Ballycotton Bay on the southeast coast. The air was fresh and the pace of life was much slower than in London. The men who fished provided the local community with an abundance of seafood. The farmers who cultivated the land grew vegetables and prepared meat, such as lamb and beef. There was a natural spirit and humble pride in the people who lived there.

The years during World War II often kept Philip and his wife, Lucy, from traveling between London and Ireland. At the time, Shanagarry—like many isolated communities all over Ireland—lacked modern health-care facilities, so Lucy decided to give birth to her children in London, where she could be assured of the best hospital care. After the war ended, Simon was born in London in 1946, where he spent the first four years of his life. In 1950, Philip moved his family permanently to Ireland.

Philip was a cultured man who loved art, music, and books, and he was also keenly interested in design. On the edge of a marsh overlooking Ballycotton Bay, he built a modern house with large glass windows to absorb the light and expansive views of the bay. Lucy and Philip were discriminating in their choice of furniture and housewares, choosing chairs of contemporary Scandinavian design, new stainless-steel flatware by Danish design company Georg Jensen, and the best copper cooking pots from Sweden. But they also revered and collected many of the local traditional crafts, such as woven market baskets, ironwork, and earthenware pottery.

Miles of unpaved roads still prevail around Shanagarry, where as a child Simon rode his bicycle to seek out friends and adventures.

OPPOSITE
The lighthouse on the island at Ballycotton Bay is an iconic landmark. In the spring, the gorse bush is in full bloom along the rocky-ledged cliffs that lead down to the sea. It is here that Simon and his childhood friends had a favorite swimming hole.

FOLLOWING SPREAD
The wall and gate at the back of Kilmahon House, Simon's childhood home. The building in the foreground was originally the horse stable; Simon's father renovated it to become the pottery.

The front entrance to Kilmahon House as it looked when the Pearce family lived there.

A small, traditional earthenware pitcher with yellow glaze by Philip Pearce. Collection Simon Pearce

A Shanagarry Pottery mug, designed by Philip Pearce, remains unchanged after fifty years in production.

OPPOSITE
The remains of a typical nineteenth-century Irish farm cottage on the southern coast of County Cork.

Throughout the long, rainy winters, Simon, as a young child, awoke to the deep moaning sounds of the lighthouse foghorn. In the summers, he picked blackberries that covered the *borines* (the long paths that led down to the sea). He rode his bicycle down the narrow country lanes to play with his childhood friends and often stayed with neighbors on overnight visits. Back then, all around the bay there were many stone and plaster cottages, with a few modest rooms, and oftentimes six to a dozen children in a family shared a bedroom. Ireland was a poor country in the 1950s and most men in Shanagarry were making the equivalent of about five dollars or less a week. Families stretched their finances and had to be practical out of necessity to survive. A spirit of resourcefulness prevailed in the people, who managed by doing things themselves. In contrast to the economic hardships, Simon recalls that there was always a feeling of safety and welcomeness in a neighbor's home.

Philip decided to become a farmer and went into partnership with his friend, Ivan Allen, at the Allen farm in the nearby village of Ballymaloe. Philip refurbished a wing of the Allen's house and moved his family there. He also renovated several outbuildings, restored pastures, built glass greenhouses, researched crops, and helped Allen make the farm flourish. The farm eventually grew to become Ballymaloe House, home of its namesake restaurant, created by Ivan's wife, Myrtle Allen, and expanded to a nearby property as the renowned Ballymaloe Cookery School and Gardens, created by their daughter-in-law, Darina Allen. After a few years, Philip decided he did not want to farm; instead he followed his dream to become a potter. Leaving Ballymaloe House and the considerable time and resources he had put into it, he bought an old property and former rectory, Kilmahon House, a Georgian villa and gardens, where he turned a horse stable into a pottery. It was here that Simon learned how to make pots, and his appreciation for making things by hand began.

Willie Greene, an elderly potter with vast knowledge and skill from nearby Youghal, spent months at Kilmahon House and taught Philip to make pots in the traditional earthenware style of the region. Philip also trained with English master potter Harry Davis (1910–1986) at his Crowan Pottery studio in Cornwall, England, in 1952, learning glaze techniques. Davis was an early protégé of Bernard Leach (1887–1979), the English potter who founded the legendary Leach Pottery in St. Ives, Cornwall, England, in 1920. Philip made functional ware: plates, pitchers, mugs, bowls, cups, and vases. Simon and his brother, Stephen, helped out in the pottery preparing clay and glazes and packing

The weather changes often on Ballycotton Bay, a space so expansive and visible that a storm can rage on the sea while the sun shines on the land.

The marsh between Kilmahon House and the sea where Simon often hunted.

Ireland's sheep are often contained in high stone-wall-lined pastures. Many of the walls are centuries old.

OPPOSITE
The rugged landscape of Ireland's western shores is prime grazing territory for sheep.

FOLLOWING SPREAD
A typical trout stream in the remote region of County Kerry, where Simon often headed for weeklong camping and fishing expeditions.

the kiln. Simon often rode on a tractor sixteen miles to Youghal to dig clay in an old clay field at an abandoned pottery where Willie Greene had once worked. He returned to the family workshop hours later with as much raw clay as he could fit into the wagon. Simon learned the skill of throwing pots, and his contribution added to the pottery's production.

Philip trained a few local men to become potters, and his workshop became a small working pottery, which he named Shanagarry Pottery. Putting local tradition aside, Philip's desire grew to design pottery that would have his signature contemporary look. He developed a new range of pottery, distinguished by its modern forms and bold black-and-white glazes. The workshop became highly regarded for its quality design. An independent Scandinavian council reporting on design in Ireland acknowledged Philip's pottery for design excellence.[1]

Simon's mother, Lucy, lent a critical eye to the design of the pots as well as to the business. She was also an excellent cook, who believed that good nutrition is integral to the mind and body functioning well. She, too, was resourceful and taught herself to cook by reading articles and books by food writers of the time such as Elizabeth David, who through her food section newspaper articles introduced Mediterranean food to Irish readers and later wrote books on French and Italian cuisine. Each day Lucy cooked traditional Irish meals for the potters to provide them with nutritionally balanced lunches, and she prepared Italian- or French-style meals for the family each evening. Lucy made sure that gathering around the table at lunch and dinner was an important time to relax, eat well, and socialize.

Simon's life in Shanagarry was a mix of different worlds. His parents were from London, they were educated and cultured, and they embraced country life. The local Irish people were rooted in traditional country ways; they were strong and resourceful. It was a safe and worry-free place to grow up. As a child, Simon often accompanied Tommy Sliney, a Ballycotton fishmonger, twice each week to sell fish to his customers from a cart drawn by a donkey. In Ballycotton today, an old photograph of Sliney and his donkey hangs in the pub at the Inn by the Harbor overlooking the sea. When he wasn't in school or working in the pottery, Simon spent most of his time outdoors roaming the open land, pastures, woodlands, marsh, and seashore. He found the tranquility and solitude comforting. Simon rode his bicycle for miles to explore neighboring towns, meet up with friends, fish a favorite trout stream, or swim in the sea. To get to the other side of the bay faster than by land on bicycle, he built his own speedboat and an

outboard motor to carry him across the water.

A few old-timers often took Simon hunting. They gathered in the early morning at a cottage for a cup of tea in front of a cozy fire, and then hunted pheasant and small game in all kinds of weather, and they often fished together. With a pouch full of success over his shoulder, Simon headed home, where his mother prepared a hearty lunch from his spoils. When he was in his teens, he traveled farther with friends to the counties on the west coast, where the ruggedness of a timeless landscape and the wildness of the mountains and lakes attracted him. Around the rugged hills and mountain ranges in Country Cork and as far as County Kerry, he easily found secluded places where he camped, fished, hunted, and cooked on an open fire. It was here that Simon's love of the outdoors flourished. The land and sea offered him endless opportunities for exploration and adventure; the vast spaces of the unspoiled west coast provided him with the time for contemplation. The rawness of such experiences enriched him with an appreciation of the simplicity and directness of nature.

In Simon's parents' home, the kitchen table was an important gathering place that provided social times between the intervals of daily activities. The utilitarian objects on and around the table were quiet partners: "We never really talked about the objects on or around the table—although many of them were so beautiful and well designed—they were just there. We loved them, but never made a big deal about them."

Simon's parents had an appreciation for good design—traditional, classic, and modern—and their quest to make a livelihood from their own handmade pottery inspired similar taste and ambition in their son. Simon loved Ballycotton Bay and believed he would live in Shanagarry for the rest of his life, work at the family pottery, and continue to embrace the outdoors. Then, when Simon was sixteen he moved on his own to New Zealand to advance his pottery skills and spent two years training under English potter Harry Davis (whom Simon's father, Philip, had also trained under), who had moved from Cornwall, England, to found the Crewenna Pottery near Nelson. Under Davis's tutelage Simon's level of craftsmanship increased. When he moved back to Ireland, he worked a year with his father and brother at Shanagarry Pottery before setting up a pottery in Shanagarry under his own name, Simon Pearce Pottery. But he also yearned to create something on his own that reflected his own vision.

The city held a different kind of appeal for Simon. He often visited Patrick Scott, an architect, designer, and artist who was a great friend of Simon's parents, in Dublin. Scott, Simon's

The living room in Patrick Scott's house and studio in Dublin. In the far left corner is his cabinet of Georgian glass.

The display of old glass and pottery in the dining room at the Dublin home of artist Patrick Scott was for Simon an important influence, a source of history and design, and an example of collecting.

In Scott's bedroom a painting by the artist hangs over his desk.

OPPOSITE
A cabinet full of Irish and old Georgian glass in the Dublin home of artist Patrick Scott. It was here that Simon began to appreciate the quality of early handmade glass and yearned to make glass with a similar feeling.

godfather, was also an avid antiques collector, and among his many collections was Irish glass. Most of the glass was stored in a big wooden cupboard in the corner of the living room in Scott's house, formerly a carriage house on an alley at the back of a grand Georgian townhouse that Scott had renovated to become his home and painting studio.

Scott, who became one of Ireland's most notable modern artists, was deeply interested in the Irish Georgian era. Period furnishings, decorative arts collections, and glass in his Dublin home reflect his love of this time. When architectural design and the arts flourished during the successive reign of the four King Georges in England (1714–1830), that period in Ireland was also one of great distinction, a time often referred to as the Irish Renaissance. Goods of remarkable and distinctive craftsmanship were being produced in disciplines as diverse as plasterwork, joinery, wrought iron, stonework, silver, glass, pottery, and porcelain.[2] Simon loved to roam the neighborhoods in Dublin with endless rows of Georgian townhouses and other parts of the city that had humbler versions in the tradition of great Georgian architecture. He admired the brick facades, grand windows, and decorative doorways. He also enjoyed visiting old pubs that had not changed for hundreds of years. It was in the pubs, which were largely inhabited by men, where Irish pride was expressed (and still is today) through the spontaneous singing of an Irish ballad.

Unadorned and symmetrical, Georgian design in general possesses an innate simplicity and straightforward legibility that Simon was immediately drawn to. The influences of Georgian design are also visible in country houses familiar to Simon. Kilmahon House, where Simon lived in Shanagarry, is an excellent example of pure Georgian villa architecture. And Patrick Scott managed to save an unusually well-preserved example of an Irish cottage complete with symmetry and proportion, the predominate ingredients of grander Georgian architecture . . . its simple utilitarian construction forms the perfect backdrop for Scott's collection of Irish folk furniture.[3] Through Scott's example of preserving architecture of the past, collecting, and his love of simple design and utilitarian objects, Simon, too, drew no lines between appreciating high and low art or design.

Simon was particularly enamored with Scott's Georgian glass. In Dublin, and in towns on the road to and from Shanagarry, Simon began to explore antiques shops and flea markets and, when he could find and afford them, bought old drinking vessels and wine glasses. Old glassware, made by hand and by a craftsman, had character and individuality and seemed to hold

GEORGIAN GLASS

As early as the fourteenth century, Venetian glass from Italy dominated the taste, production, and market for glassware all over Europe until the English took the lead in the early eighteenth century. For over one hundred years, during what is commonly known as the Georgian period (1714 to 1830, when four reigning kings carried the same name), England was famous for the excellent quality of the lead glass it produced, and most notable were its drinking vessels. English glassblowers followed a process similar to the one that had been practiced in Italy and in other parts of Europe for centuries, whereby a team of two or three craftsmen was responsible for making individual parts of the glass. A master created the stem (which often contained some of the finest designs and detailing), an apprentice made the foot or base, and another craftsman made the bowl and joined the pieces together. The common feature in Georgian drinking glasses is that the width of the base is slightly larger than the bowl, and the pontil mark (the mark left on the bottom of the foot after the glass is broken free from the pontil iron) is left visible, rather than removed.

In the nineteenth century, as a result of ongoing political tensions between the English and the Irish, Ireland stopped importing glass from England and set up its own major glass production facilities in Dublin, Waterford, and Cork. Following the same methods of making glass as a team by hand, each city developed its own characteristic designs, and Irish glass of the period became as celebrated as its English counterparts.

Simon, enamored with the character and feeling of Georgian glass, was determined to make glass like it and planned his workshops and glassblowing methods to produce similar qualities in his glass. Through Simon's constant development and refinement of his furnace designs (the singular engineering component that determines the quality of melted glass and its pliability) as well as the raw compositional materials (silica, lime, barium, potash, and cullet) needed to make clear glass, he developed a recipe for lead-free glass that surpasses much of the clarity, depth, and brilliance in the glassware of earlier and contemporary glassmakers.

Most of the old Georgian, French, Scandinavian, and American glassware that Simon acquired is unsigned; the only stamp of authenticity is the pontil mark left on the bottom of each glass, indicating that the glass was made by hand. The age and country of origin of the glassware can be determined by its style and quality, but for the most part, the makers' names are lost to history. Simon also chose to retain the pontil mark on the bottom of each piece and eventually made a graphic version of the mark his trademark, which he used as the Simon Pearce logo until 2013.

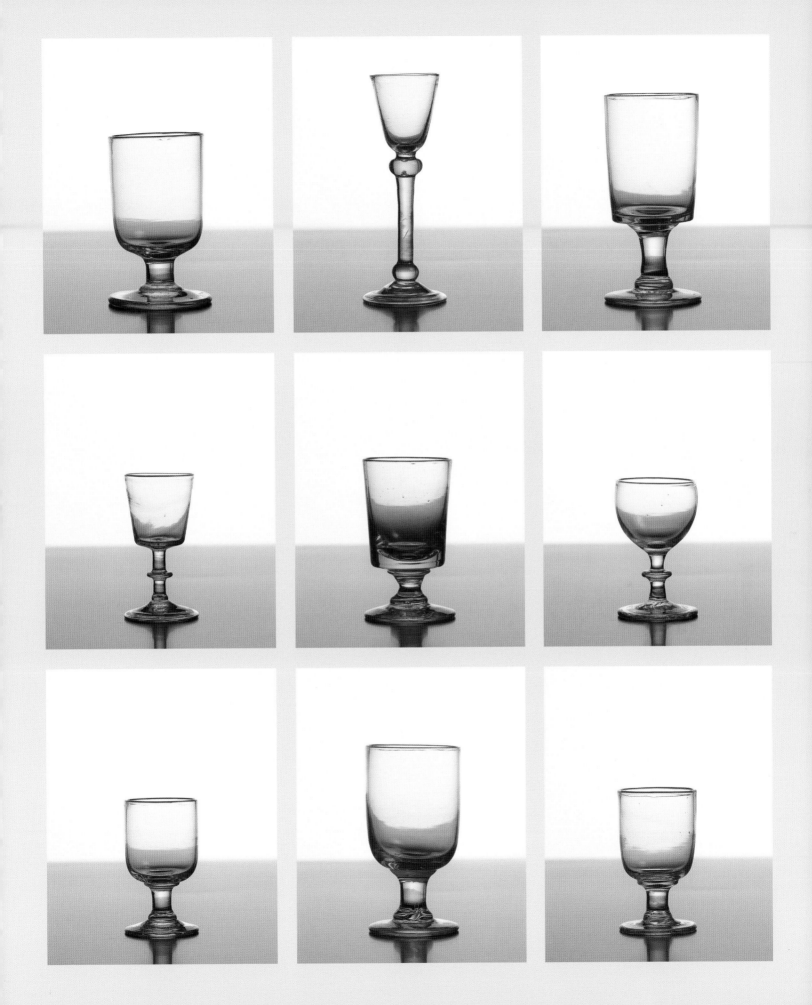

Simon's first glass, made while he was training at the Glasshouse in Covent Garden, London, 1968.

OPPOSITE
Simon at work making his Round wine glass in his Bennettsbridge workshop, 1970s.

The Simon Pearce store on Kildare Street in Dublin became a destination to see and shop for contemporary design and crafts.

The Simon Pearce store in Dublin showcased Simon's glass as well as the work of other designers and craftsmen that he carefully chose to carry. The store's interior design represented a new, clean approach to product merchandising in the 1970s. The hanging lamps in the window by Louis Poulsen are the lamps that are now installed in Simon's house in Vermont.

The Bell wine glass was one of Simon's earliest stemware designs. Now known as the Cavendish white wine glass, it remains in production today (see also pages 132–133).

OPPOSITE
The quiet, narrow lane leading to Simon's Bennettsbridge workshop and home.

light in a different way than contemporary glass. New commercial glass, made with machines, was created for uniformity and perfection; it lacked distinctive character. More than the specific shape or design, it was the simplicity of old glass that fascinated Simon. The idea of making pots out of clay gave way to the desire to make glass. Although Simon knew nothing about glassblowing, he knew he wanted to make glassware that had the feeling of the historical glass he had admired in Scott's house and the examples he was collecting. That meant studying and learning the traditional methods from the Georgian era. Glass became the pivotal shift for Simon.

Simon's love of glass paved the way for his professional career. He spent years in his quest to learn how to make glass, and it was not easy. His journey took him to schools, workshops, and factories in countries far from Ireland, including England, the Netherlands, Italy, Denmark, and Sweden. But it was to Ireland he returned with the goal of setting up his own glass workshop. In 1971, not far from Shanagarry in Bennettsbridge, County Kilkenny, he bought an old rundown cottage and outbuildings and renovated them to become his home and workshop. Like the resourceful Irish countrymen, rather than buy something new, Simon built his own furnaces and created many of the tools he needed for glassblowing. This early pattern of building furnaces, equipment, and making tools prevails in his work today. He wanted to keep his workshop small and manageable with a goal of training and employing no more than ten men and women who could produce a range of designs and a quantity consistent to meet customers' tastes and needs.

Simon spent several years perfecting his glassmaking techniques, building furnaces, and establishing a contemporary market for his glass. He opened stores in Clifden, Dublin, and Kenmare to sell his glassware. The interior of his Dublin store, an example of sleek, modern design, was an inspiration to an appreciative audience of contemporary crafts. Showcasing Simon's glassware, his father's pottery, flatware by David Mellor and Georg Jensen, and highly selected contemporary handmade Irish crafts, the Simon Pearce store in Dublin became a destination.

Simon had created a solid and growing business, but the infrastructure, bureaucracy, energy costs, and economic climate in Ireland were difficult and slow and no change was in sight. In order to achieve a new level of business goals that Simon aspired to, he would have to leave Ireland. He moved to the United States, where he found the perfect place and opportunity for establishing his workshop in Quechee, a quaint village in central Vermont.

FINDING A RIVER, MAKING A LIFE
IN VERMONT

In Vermont everyone was so helpful. I could just ask a question and I would get a response—from neighbors, people in the village, in the town—even at the State House. People were so friendly and giving when we first moved to Vermont and got started.

—SIMON PEARCE

In Ireland, Simon became frustrated and outspoken about the conditions of running a business there. As gentle and ideal a place as Ireland was to live, the administrative bureaucracies, lacking in support of economic development, seemed slow to pull the country out of a dilapidated era. The infrastructure was weak, the telephones did not work properly, traveling was slow, and electricity was frail. The availability and cost of fuel to run his furnaces was prohibitive to leading a viable business. Simon was determined to find better solutions elsewhere.

In 1980, Simon decided that he wanted to establish a glass-blowing factory and retail store in North America. He thought he might find the right place in Canada or on the East Coast of the United States. His prerequisites for the perfect location were that it had to be a beautiful place to live and work; it had to have space to establish a store; and it had to be on a river. He wanted to harness the natural energy from the moving water and convert the power to electricity to fuel his glass furnaces. Simon had thought considerably about the possibilities of hydropower; finding the river and optimum location on it was a bit more difficult.

Simon looked at several sites along the Hudson River tributaries in New York, but none of them was quite right—something was always lacking. By chance, while attending a family wedding in New England, Simon and his wife, Pia, drove north to central Vermont and the small village of Quechee to look at a two-hundred-year-old former woolen mill. When they arrived and saw the old brick building, the majestic river, and the water falling over the dam, they knew it was everything they had been looking for. In 1981, the mill in Quechee became their home and workshop.

Simon built a furnace at the old mill, and made glass along-side three Irish glassblowers he had moved from Bennettsbridge. Pia ran a small retail store, where she sold Simon's first American-made products. Work continued at the mill and people came to visit, to see glass made, and to shop at the store. Simon and Pia opened a restaurant overlooking the river, waterfall, and

Simon making a Round wine glass (now called the Essex wine glass) in his first Vermont workshop, 1981.

OPPOSITE
The river, waterfall, and cantilevered restaurant at Simon Pearce, the mill, in Quechee, Vermont, today.

The Tapered wine glass was one of Simon's new designs when he set up his workshop and store in Vermont in 1981. It is a fine example of glassware that is completely free blown, without the use of molds. In the early 1980s, the uniqueness and individual character of each piece was a new concept in the American glass market.

Simon and Pia in the Simon Pearce store at the mill in Quechee, Vermont, 1980s. Pia was in charge of establishing the retail store. In it she sought to display Simon's first American-made products alongside linens, crafts, and wood bowls, imported from Ireland. She created simple, elegant table settings to inspire customers.

quintessential covered bridge, and set tables with the glass and pottery their craftspeople made. From the kitchen, they introduced visitors to hearty Irish meals and favorite family recipes. They had created an experience for visitors, and many of them became faithful customers.

In his first product catalogue, Simon explained his work to a new American audience: "The uniqueness of each piece is particularly apparent in the round stemmed glasses. These are completely free blown. Traditional wooden moulds are used for the more rigidly shaped vessels. Each item is hand finished to give character and a feeling of softness to the glass. The tools we use, including our blowing irons and moulds, are basically unchanged in design from those used centuries ago."[4]

Vermont is known for its history and traditions and for its resourceful people. Neighbors embraced Simon and Pia's approach to renovating and revitalizing an old mill, creating well-made wares, introducing new cuisine, infusing energy into a small village, and attracting visitors to it. Vermont was different from, but not unlike, Ireland. There were similarities in the lifestyle and the benefits of country living: clean air, fresh water, open land, good food, and kind people. Simon was deeply affected by his life in Ireland and those early experiences translated to his life and work in Vermont. Where Ireland lacked in entrepreneurial support, Vermont and the United States encouraged businesses and growth and looked to the future. Simon sought help and advice and it was provided easily and honestly. Simon built a business capable of sustaining a consistent, high level of quality and production to meet demand, and his company expanded. Over the next two decades, he opened three new production facilities and stores in cities and towns in several states. His tale is similar to many American stories, where innovation and the drive to create something unique result in success. His glass designs and methods to produce them were appealing to a growing audience nationwide, proving that handmade products could compete in the marketplace.

One person—Jan (pronounced "Yahn") Mollmark—made a marked contribution to the development and success of Simon's business. Hired in 1994, Jan developed a perfect working relationship with Simon. It was through Simon's design skills and Jan's technical and engineering knowledge that their glassmaking methods matured, flourished, and opened up new possibilities for design and production.

Jan, born and raised in Sweden, knew glass well. In Sweden, the glass industry, workshops, and glassware designs were an

Simon Pearce is a designer and blower of glass. He was raised in County Cork, Ireland and began his career in glass in 1960 at The Royal College of Art in London. He worked in some of Europe's most renowned glass factories including Leerdam in Holland, Vennini in Italy, Boda and Orrefors in Sweden.

Simon established his own workshop in Kilkenny where he designed and produced his glass for ten years. His aim was to create simple, timeless and contemporary glass.

In 1981 Simon decided to move his glass-blowing operation to the United States. He bought a beautiful old woolen mill in Quechee, Vermont where his glass is made with two things in mind: beauty and function. The limited output of the workshop makes possible the use of old glassblowing techniques rarely used today. Each piece has its own distinct individual character.

The cross underneath each piece of glass is made by the pontil iron which holds the glass while the rim is hand finished. It is an integral part of the making process and is consistent with the feeling of the glass as something hand-made and personal. For this reason, it is left as the Simon Pearce trademark.

Two pages from an early 1980s Simon Pearce catalogue introduced the products to a new American audience, taking care to explain that Simon is a glass designer and maker of handmade glass. The catalogue also educated the consumer about the importance of the pontil mark, which he registered as his trademark. Success in the United States came quickly and Simon began to open Simon Pearce stores in towns and cities on the East Coast.

SIMON PEARCE
THE MILL, QUECHEE
VERMONT 05059

TEL 802 295-2711

SIMON PEARCE
39 MAIN STREET
FREEPORT, ME 04032

TEL 207 865-0464

SIMON PEARCE
385 BLEECKER STREET
NEW YORK, NY 10014

TEL 212 924-1142

47

Free-blown glass bowl made at the Kosta glass factory in Kosta, Sweden, 1821.

Hand-blown glass vases with turned-over rims designed by Edward Hald for Orrefors Glasbruk, Orrefors, Sweden, 1940s.

Glass bowl with blue rim, Denmark, circa 1850. Collection Simon Pearce. Denmark, like Sweden, had its own glass culture, which was particularly vibrant from 1825 to 1925.

OPPOSITE
Simon's Round vases as shown in his first Vermont catalogue, 1981. His goal in his marketing materials was to show his glass as simply and as objectively as possible to allow an appreciation of the forms, contours, transparency, and handmade quality of his designs.

integral part of the social and cultural framework. Swedes made glass by hand and revered it for its design and quality. Jan recalls when he was a boy that oftentimes women and children would bring lunch to the glassblowers and they would all sit outdoors at long wooden tables and have lunch together. Glass was so much a part of the country's social fabric that during the long, cold winters, homeless people were allowed to spend nights in the glass factories to keep warm.

In the first half of the twentieth century in Småland, the forested region where the majority of the glass factories in Sweden were located, within a fifty-mile radius there were perhaps eighty to ninety factories. When machine-made glass was introduced in the late 1950s, the traditional glass factories were threatened by mechanical efficiency and the speed of production. These factories began to close, and by 2000 there were only a handful left. Orrefors (established in 1898), the most famous of all glassmakers in the world, shuttered its doors in 2012. Today, only two factories are left in Sweden: Kosta (established in 1742) and Målerås (established in 1890). A few small-scale glassmaking studios produce limited hand-finished products to a local clientele, but the economic challenges of running a large furnace and making handmade glass on a large scale is too challenging; the glass culture in Sweden is now a thing of the past. Similar stories of the decline of the glass industry are prevalent in other European countries. To meet the steep demand for lower-priced glassware, the quality suddenly diminished. Today, fine glass is still produced on a large scale by Waterford Crystal (established in 1783) in Waterford, Ireland, and Baccarat (established in 1764) in Baccarat, France. However, both company's products are largely machine finished.

When he was just five years old, in 1949, Jan often visited the Strömbergshyttan glass factory in Småland, where his father worked as a glassblower and his mother signed and numbered glassware. During his summer vacations when he was ten, he began helping out at the factory. In 1957, at fourteen, Jan left school to start his glassblowing training at Strömbergshyttan. As his interest ran to the technical side of glassmaking, he focused on engineering. Later, as an adult, Jan earned a degree in mechanical engineering. Eventually, he made glass molds in graphite, cast iron, and wood and worked closely with glass designers to translate their designs into three-dimensional samples, which were made by the glassblowers. In 1972, he began work with Ugnasbyggnadsbryån, a Swedish furnace company, and understood that one of the most important technical priorities in glassmaking is the quality of the furnace—it ultimately has everything to do with

No. 610 Large Round Vase
H 14"   W 4½"

No. 656 Medium Round Vase
H 11"   W 3¾"

3

Technical engineer Jan Mollmark (right) demonstrates to Simon the way a new steel mold works to make a glass bowl under design development.

A glassblower at the Simon Pearce facility in Windsor, Vermont, heats a gather of glass in a melting furnace.

A glassblower at the Simon Pearce facility in Quechee, Vermont, blows a gather of glass.

OPPOSITE
Clothing and furnaces have changed over the centuries, but the process of blowing glass and hand finishing it have been practiced in the same way for hundreds of years. From Diderot's *Encyclopédie*, 1751–72 (top) and at the Simon Pearce workshop in Windsor, Vermont, 2015 (bottom).

the absolute quality of glass—its ability to be formed, its clarity, and its brilliance. In 1974, he left Sweden to work for Dartington Crystal in Torrington, England, where he stayed for eighteen years, and at Edinburgh Crystal in Scotland from 1993 to 1994.

Simon had been searching for an experienced technical engineer for his Vermont glassmaking company and recruited Jan, who was put in charge of running production, working on the melting glass furnaces, and making molds, the forms in which glass is blown. Jan improved machine tooling, the devices for shaping rigid materials; and the glory holes, the small furnaces used to keep glass pliable so that it can be worked. He also integrated sandblasting and introduced the centrifuge process—a rapidly rotating machine that applies centrifugal force to liquid glass. Due to Jan's expertise, Simon's glass production became more efficient. Jan introduced innovative methods. Impressed with Simon's knowledge of furnaces, Jan said, "Simon has made twenty furnaces, and they are the best I have seen." Since moving to Vermont, Jan has refurbished five furnaces with Simon, and has taken on this work as his chief responsibility.

Over the next two decades, Simon designed new glass each year and brought his drawings to Jan. Due to his experience in Sweden and England, Jan was expert at transforming drawings into three-dimensional samples. As the chief collaborator in implementing Simon's designs, Jan said, "It is important to work closely between design and the technical aspects of making glass to achieve a better success rate. Simon was very responsive to my skills and our process of working together because he knew glassblowing himself. It was very easy to work with him." In the many years Jan has worked with glass designers, he found that "they were all trained in art schools—not one was a glassmaker— Simon is the only one who is a maker, the only one who understands glass design and how to make it."

"Glass is in my blood," said Jan. He has witnessed firsthand the decline of an industry that was part of his heritage, but notes that in the fifty-five years he has worked in glass, there hasn't been a substantial change in the way factories that he has chosen to work in because each continues to follow the same time-honored processes of handmade glass. He adds, "Today, other than in small studios, no one else in the world is making glass the way Simon Pearce does."

Fig. 2.

The Ship's carafe was designed in Ireland and produced for many years in Vermont. The gentle fold of glass at the base of the neck expresses the fluidity of the glass material as well as makes visible the two gathers of glass needed to make the piece.

In Ireland, Simon designed three sizes for the cylindrical Bud vase, which allowed creative displays of repeat and varied sizes. Designed to display single or a few flowers, its modern look broke away from some of Simon's more traditional designs.

The Trumpet wine glass combines classic Georgian design and form with Simon's own characteristic sensitivity to volume and contour. He interpreted an old concept and made it new (see also pages 130–131).

OPPOSITE
The simplicity of line and the thickness and weight of the glass in the Shelburne vase exemplify Simon's iconic style (see also pages 206–207).

INNOVATION AND ICONIC STYLE FOR EVERYDAY GLASS

When I started making glass my intention was to make pleasing, simple glasses for everyday use. The designs would be timeless and would hold up to constant use, and not chip or break easily.

—SIMON PEARCE

Handmade glass has been blown in certain ways and in a variety of traditional shapes for thousands of years. The differences appearing over time are not as dramatic as, say, the pencil is to the computer. Simon chose to apply traditional methods of blowing glass honoring the qualities of old glassware, but he also wanted to express his personal aesthetic for a contemporary market. He created new forms by constantly simplifying line, form, and volume. By continually rebuilding and improving his tools, furnaces, and processes, Simon brought innovation to glassmaking.

Simon's true success as a designer comes from the fact that he is first of all a maker. His experience in making things began in early childhood when he fabricated parts to repair his bicycle, or later as a potter in his teens in his father's pottery as he made many clay mugs, pitchers, and bowls. The time required to become proficient and skilled in making pottery and in blowing glass cannot be underestimated. As Simon said in 1976 in an article he wrote for *Crafts* magazine, "Perhaps it is the repetition which I believe is inevitable in the learning of almost every craft and perhaps I was lucky that when I started making pottery I trained in a workshop environment where you just took it for granted that you had to spend the first years going through this sort of apprenticeship stage; just doing repetitive production work, before you really started doing anything seriously of your own. For me it's certainly one of the most satisfying experiences, coming through the stages, whether it is glass or pottery. Firstly the basic grasping of the skill, then being able to make two the same, then getting the rhythm and speed better and always trying something a little harder, so you hardly feel you are improving, until you go back to the very simple things and this gives you a great feeling of control and satisfaction."[5]

Design as a purely intellectual or aesthetic pursuit alone held no interest for Simon; his goal was to make something useful, beautiful, and lasting. As the English design guru Terence Conran said, "Good design is really intelligence made visible. . . . Good design tends to be enduring."[6] Once Simon gained experience and

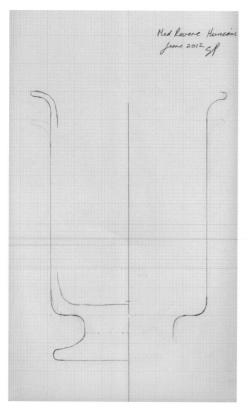

Med Revere Hurricane
June 2012 SP

Once Simon settles on developing a design, he draws its contours on graph paper, constantly perfecting the positive and negative space on the outside and inside shapes. Note by the erasure how he decided to increase the height of the hurricane during the drawing phase. Based on this kind of drawing, Jan Mollmark oversees the next step in the development of the design, a three-dimensional sample.

Today, glassblowers in three Simon Pearce workshops are responsible for making glassware. They utilize a variety of methods to achieve the quality and look and feeling of handmade glass.

OPPOSITE
A page from one of Simon's sketchbooks. He uses his sketches to record his immediate thoughts and ideas. Returning to his books later, he will decide to eliminate some concepts and to develop others.

confidence as a glassmaker, he was able to transition to become a glass designer. For him, both endeavors are equally important; it is this rare combination that contributes to the exemplary reputation of his products today.

Simon's design process is simple. In the early days in Ireland when he had an idea in his head he made things: "Like the Essex wine glass, which we still make after forty-three years, I just made it—free blown. It was the shape of the glass I wanted and as I blew it I added a stem and a foot. So that is a really good example of design while you are making."

Today, his designs for new glassware often start with a quick sketch on paper, followed by a profile drawing, similar to an architectural elevation. Simon admits that drawing does not come naturally to him, but the act of committing ideas on paper creates a helpful reference. Days, months, or years after he makes a sketch in his notebooks, Simon may revisit an idea, which is then developed into its three-dimensional form. (He never works on a computer or with 3-D software programs to design glass.) For his process and vision, he uses his hands and the simplest tools to realize his design goals.

Historically, wood or steel molds were introduced to the glassmaking process to ensure uniformity, efficiency, and speed. There are inherent limitations in making blown glass with the old methods, but Simon always advocates the use of a combination of molds, free blowing, and whatever techniques, tools, or equipment he and his glassblowers might need to achieve the end result. The process, however, is still very low-tech, and although Simon and his longtime collaborator Jan Mollmark have developed and perfected innovative molds, machinery, and devices to create glass, the process remains remarkably similar to the glass-blowing techniques that were in practice hundreds of years ago.

The clarity of glass is the direct result of the quality of the raw materials, the sophistication of the glass furnace, and the pace at which the molten glass moves through the furnace and into production. The glass must be used and worked fairly quickly. If it sits for long periods of time and is not stimulated, the quality and workability of it deteriorates. Simon has always been devoted to only making clear glass and his choice to do so is in great part an aesthetic preference: "I work in clear glass as almost everything I make is functional and for me the main virtue and beauty of glass is its transparency, being able to see what is contained, be it a glass of red wine or a bowl of colorful fruit."[7]

Simon never wanted to replicate designs from the past. Bridging history and contemporary moments are important to him.

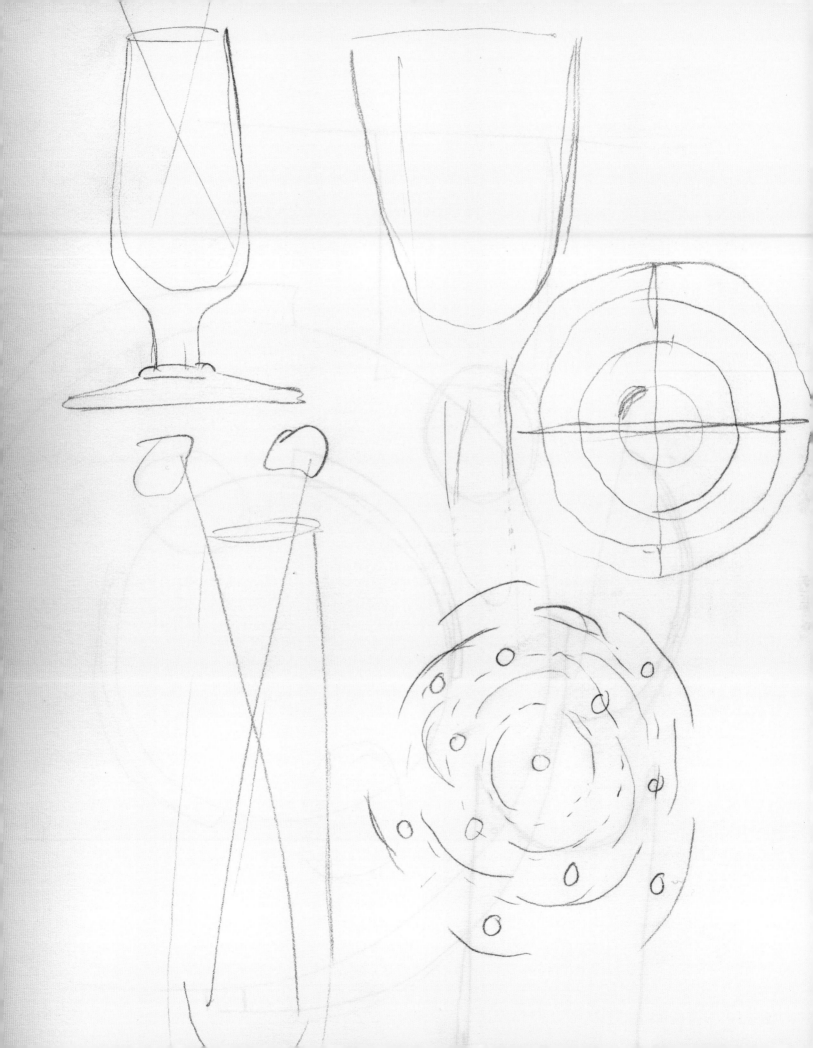

Stemware from Simon's collection of Georgian glass.

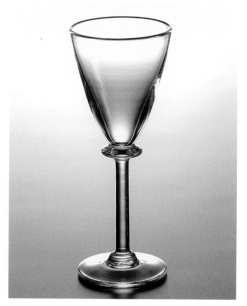

Simon's Cavendish white wine glass (see also pages 132–133).

Simon's Hartland goblet is a design extension of his Hartland white wine glass (see also pages 134–135).

OPPOSITE
Essex wine glass (see also pages 128–129).

However, historical references to Georgian glassware are apparent in three of Simon's stemware designs. Each of these classic Simon Pearce designs hark back to the traditions of old glass that Simon reveres. The Essex wine glass (originally called the Round wine glass) is one of the first glasses Simon designed and produced in Ireland—it remains his most popular glass today. The simple, straight-sided shape of the bowl is reminiscent of old pub glasses. Simon designed the stem to be more substantial than historical examples and added a simple detail around the collar. The thickness of the glass not only provides a distinctive personality but also captures and holds light with more luminosity than thin glass. The thickness also makes it exceptionally durable; it feels less flimsy, will hold up to use, and will last a long time.

Simon realized that the successful design of Essex represents everything that was essential to his personal vision. "Everything about it worked—the weight, size, and proportions—the 'everything' is right there in that glass." He notes that the Essex is versatile—it works not only for water, beer, gin and tonic, and wine but also as an ice-cream bowl or a vase. The multipurpose quality of the Essex had popular appeal, and his customers were eager for more pieces in this vein.

The Bell wine glass (now called the Cavendish wine glass) was originally created in Ireland, and it, too, was carried over into production in Vermont. Drinking white wine out of a cone-shaped glass rather than a ball-shaped bowl is a European tradition—the Cavendish design pays homage to that custom. It has a thinner stem and a larger cone-shaped bowl than its Georgian counterpart. The Cavendish glass became successful in the United States in part because of its unusual shape, and the market craze for white wine in the early 1980s. Simon was keenly aware of the market demand for a more traditional red wine glass too. So he created the Woodstock balloon wine glass, which has a fuller bowl and a closed top in order to allow a red wine's bouquet to be appreciated, as well as glasses for a few of its wine-specific varietal cousins.

Simon's Hartland glass is perhaps the most decorative of his stemware designs. Again, drawing on a Georgian practice, where the Irish glass master created a stem with distinctive personality, Simon designed a very simple glass bowl and base but added a glass ball under the collar to give it an ornate twist. The Hartland glass, like the Essex, is a vessel that can be used for a variety of beverages. By the early 1990s, Simon Pearce glassware was synonymous with sophisticated design, a high level of craftsmanship, and usability.

Simon's Woodbury vases are noted for their square shapes and hand-finished rims and edges (see also pages 208–209).

The square Woodbury pitcher is one of Simon's most innovative and successful designs (see also pages 152–153).

OPPOSITE
The square Woodbury bowl is perhaps Simon's most significant contribution to glass design (see also pages 174–175).

Throughout the history of glassmaking, designs evolved as a result of technical developments. Sometimes when glassblowers worked on a specific aspect of a piece, they might alter the technique and something unexpected and pleasing would come out of their experimentation; the experiment would become a discovery—a result of the technique versus a preconceived idea. For Simon, his Woodbury bowl is a perfect example of this creative process.

Noted for its simple square shape, the Woodbury bowl is considered an icon of modern glass design and is the most popular object Simon has created. His love of the natural world and chance are an important part of its story. The precursor to the Woodbury bowl is his Square vase. Its square shape was not revolutionary, as glassmakers had been making square vases for decades. But in Simon's mind they were all too perfect—the edges were perfect, the corners were perfect, the rims were perfect—because they were formed, cut, and machine polished and they looked very rigid. Simon wanted "to make a square vase that was very soft looking, where there was movement on the walls, and movement on the top, especially. With a hand-finished rim you won't find a perfect flat, sharp, edge of cut glass. Instead, you get a nice soft edge, with a little bit of movement and a little bit of unevenness. Even in the shape coming down the wall you can see variation and movement. You can actually feel it. So it's a very different look and feel than a commercial or a mass-produced square vase." One of Simon's most popular vases, it was eventually named the Woodbury vase.

Woodbury is one of Simon's most unique and successful collections. Simon designed several objects for this line: For the Square pitcher, based on his Square vase, he altered the vase's proportions so that it was lower and wider. One corner of the square became the lip, so that the vase could readily pour, and he designed a flat handle at the corner opposite the lip. His Square pitcher was a new concept in the marketplace and it became an immediate and lasting success. The Woodbury bowl appears to be simple but in actuality is quite complex. It is a clear example of how the act of making a difficult piece created its unique design. Originally, the bowl was to have a flat top. When the square form was opened, centrifugal force combined with the intense heat of the fire in the glory hole formed a natural flare on the top four sides of the bowl. To Simon's surprise, an unexpected, graceful curve emerged, one that had a natural flow rather than looking forced or cut. As soon as he saw it, he loved it. By chance, he had hit on something that was unique and part of the natural process

of making an object, and the results proved to be more interesting than what he had imagined and had drawn on paper. Simon is modest about his discovery and originality: "I've never seen anything remotely similar to our square bowl. And that used to be a big deal in early days of original design; now it isn't. Because that's not what's important; making something that you really are pleased with, and what pleases you is, I think, much more important than being original."

Simon also wanted to explore creating decorative objects that had no obvious function. He settled on the idea of making a glass tree but it became an unexpected challenge. Indeed, this project went beyond the scope of his methodology. He had a year of unsuccessful attempts and was close to giving up when, finally, an idea dawned on him, which was to cut hot molten glass with steel shears. It resulted in success. Like the Woodbury bowl, Simon's glass trees are an example of the ability to let go of a rigid adherence to established design processes. Just as each tree in nature is different, it is impossible to make two identical glass trees fashioned by this technique. Each is hand sculpted from start to finish and every branch is individually cut. The trees are whimsical, and when a number of them are grouped together, they create an enchanted forest.

DESIGN: THE BEAUTY OF IMPERFECTION

When you have a piece that's absolutely perfect, it feels to me like a human being had nothing to do with it. Perfection is about controlling—by mechanism, by machine, by the mold, by whatever. But as soon as there's movement and light variation, then there's a human quality to it. That, to me, is why I started making glass: because of that humanness, that human quality you find in real handmade glass.

—SIMON PEARCE

Simon's innate grasp of the glass medium comes directly from his experience making pottery and glass. However, in developing his own glass designs he was influenced by industrial design and handmade crafts. He recognized the differences between these two disciplines and melded aspects of each. In general, industrial design tends to advocate perfection and consistent replication; handmade crafts, in particular pottery, are all about the individual touch. Simon invites a subtle degree of variability and

Simon's design of the Vermont Evergreen is the result of its innovative process (see also pages 222–223).

OPPOSITE
Simon designed a glass tankard in Ireland and the same design is in production today; its form is based on early pewter tankards used in Irish and English pubs. The glassmaking process ensures a certain degree of individuality and imperfection, which many recognize as inherent beauty.

A pot made by Lucie Rie, one of the several potters whose work Simon appreciates for its quality (see also pages 244–245).

Simon has collected many examples of work by English potter Michael Cardew (see also pages 242–243).

English potter Richard Batterham is well known for his distinctive pots and range of functional ware (see also pages 254–255).

OPPOSITE
Simon's free-blown glasses offer clear references to his love of Georgian glassware and illustrate the uniqueness of each piece and the subtleties and imperfections inherent in their shapes and surfaces.

individuality in his pieces. It is the nuances in handmade glass—in form and texture—that make his work celebrated.

In Ireland, "design" was not a familiar term to Simon; he was exposed to a world of makers and there was a strong element of practicality that came with makers: "I grew up on a farm and there was always someone doing something or making something. And the actual 'design' word was never really used. The farmers made fences and walls. My father made pottery. My mother always made things; she cooked and made clothes for herself and even started a children's clothing business. My parents always looked out for Irish crafts because the traditions were dying off: woolens that were woven on looms, baskets that were handmade, and metalwork that was forged. People just simply made beautiful things as opposed to designed them."

The traditional handmade crafts that Simon knew as a boy were primarily utilitarian, and as he grew older he became aware that handmade objects bridged utility and artistry. Such potters as Harry Davis, Michael Cardew, and Lucie Rie employed traditional throwing methods but their work was much more sophisticated and refined than the work of rural crafts folk. When Simon was nineteen and he returned home from his pottery training in New Zealand, he became aware of this exciting world of potters. English potter Richard Batterham's work was another example that bridged both worlds; he was making one-of-a-kind pieces, specifically large vases and bowls, in addition to mugs, soup bowls, and plates for everyday use. While impressed by the artistry of these potters, Simon chose to create functional objects, which still possess "humanness."

The element of personal touch became an essential factor in Simon's work. The Woodbury vase is perhaps the clearest example that exemplifies his goals. It has a solid, heavy base and thick walls and rim so that when it is heated and hand finished, it possesses a lovely roundness on top that is similar, but different enough, each time. The softness that results from the process is what he likes. The process of making the vase allows a great degree of nuance and individuality to come through: "If you've got a group of them together, they're all slightly different; some have a flare, some are pretty dead straight. That's all part of it. That's how it should be. I don't want them all identical. I don't want them all trying to be perfect."

On the other hand, Simon was able as a maker to appreciate the sophistication and precision of industrial design. Viewing a humble handmade wicker basket or a piece of old earthenware pottery next to "the most beautiful, contemporary Swedish-designed

Simon's recent design for a vase expresses "humanness" through free blowing and shaping the glass by hand; the flow and movement that appear on the glass walls could never be replicated in the same way by a machine.

Simon originally designed this small glass for his granddaughter. The size and undulating shape of the glass allows a child to easily hold it. The dimpled texture dances with light. Known as the Woodbury glass, it can also be used by adults as a whiskey glass. Versatility is an important goal of Simon's designs.

Simon's recent vase design is a clear example of free-blown glassware that is not perfect; it celebrates the beauty of imperfection and individual character.

OPPOSITE
Simon's iteration of his Essex wine glass is part of his constant exploration of his first and classic glass form. This sample exemplifies the beauty of individuality in his free-blown glasses.

stainless-steel pots and pans with copper bottoms and their absolutely perfect shapes and lines," which he says, "are incredibly functional and beautiful to look at," there was never a thought that one was better or right. The common denominator is beauty and utility.

Simon does not identify himself as a religious person. He relates to the practice of "mindfulness," a philosophy and practice closely associated with Buddhist traditions. Simon's interest in Eastern thought helped him to appreciate ancient Korean, Chinese, Japanese, and Vietnamese pottery. The imperfect beauty and character of simple forms are well rooted in the wide range of humble utilitarian pottery that Simon made an effort to see in museum collections during his travels.

There are two Japanese terms that are often specifically associated with ancient Asian pottery that come close to capturing the elusive qualities that Simon admires. The term *mingei,* coined by pottery collector and scholar Sōetsu Yanagi, who authored the book *The Unknown Craftsman: A Japanese Insight into Beauty,* published in 1972, elevates ancient Korean utilitarian pottery as works of art. Even though they were made by unknown craftspeople for ordinary people to use every day, they have an intrinsic beauty. In *mingei,* beauty lies in simple form, clay material, and glazing technique. Another Eastern concept is Japan's *wabi-sabi.* There is no direct English translation. At its core, it is an appreciation of natural simplicity and timelessness, where the past is present today, and the present lives in the past and future. *Wabi-sabi* celebrates the allure of individual character. Objects made by hand are closer to the *wabi-sabi* way of being than objects made by machines. No machine can compare with a man's hands. Machinery gives speed, power, complete uniformity, and precision, but lacks individuality. The human hand is the ever-present tool of human feeling.[8] The descriptive qualities that resonate in *wabi-sabi* are closely aligned with Simon's glass, as it is in much of the pottery and the lives of the potters, such as Shoji Hamada, Richard Batterham, and Gwyn Hanssen Pigott, whose work Simon takes great interest in seeing and collecting. For Simon, it is not just the importance of designing pleasing shapes and forms for an intended use. It is the impact that simple, graceful objects can make in our lives. It is this visual and tactile quality that handmade objects especially possess.

DESIGN FOR LIVING

"Beautiful" and "functional" are the two words Simon expressed as his earliest goals in designing and making glassware; he has consistently held on to these objectives for well over forty years. As a child in Ireland, Simon appreciated the comfort and significance of the table as a gathering place for meals and the social times it provided. The objects his parents placed on the table were thoughtfully chosen. These early impressions remain important to him to this day. The home that Simon and his wife, Pia, have created for themselves in Vermont, with its lush gardens surrounded by verdant fields and woodlands, inspires Simon's designs. His desire to create glass with individuality and character inspires others to compose inviting moments with glass that are simple, sophisticated, and beautiful, whether a table setting or a vase of flowers in an entryway.

AT HOME IN VERMONT

Pia and Simon Pearce's home in Vermont is a visible expression of their love of living in the country, where breathing clean air, gardening, growing vegetables, cooking meals, and gathering around the table with family and friends come together in a comfortable blend of simplicity and attention to design. Experiences outdoors are equally important to experiences indoors. Outdoors, the serene landscape replete with vegetable and flower gardens creates an awareness of the changing seasons. The interiors are an eclectic mix of antique Irish country and modernist American and Scandinavian furniture. The materials and colors in the rooms are natural and subdued. Old wood in a variety of warm hues is set against lightly pigmented walls. Objects and artwork are sensitively arranged. The couple's friends made most of the pottery, textiles, and artwork they have collected over many years. Old European and American glass has been placed on shelves and cabinets that also display Simon's creations. Everything is meant to be used and to be enjoyed.

OPPOSITE
An antique Irish dresser in Pia and Simon's kitchen is filled with an assortment of Simon Pearce glass and Richard Batterham pottery.

Design is always carefully considered at Pia and Simon's home in Vermont. Two large terra-cotta pots flank the outside "mudroom" entrance off the cobblestone courtyard.

OPPOSITE
The quiet country road leading to the Pearce's home.

A nineteenth-century
Vermont wrought-iron
fire tool rests against
the stone fireplace.

OPPOSITE
In a large room
constructed from an old
post-and-beam barn
frame are Simon Pearce
Silver Lake hurricanes
on the mantel; above
them is artwork by
Patrick Scott. On an
antique French side
table is a glass lamp by
Simon. The Cottage
side chairs are by
Charles Shackleton,
and the curtains were
woven in Ireland at
Kerry Woollen Mills,
in Killarney.

A large floor-to-ceiling window in the Pearce's kitchen provides an uninterrupted view of the land outdoors.

OPPOSITE
An Irish Georgian wine glass from Simon's collection.

Old exterior barn boards have been cleaned and installed indoors on many of the walls of Pia and Simon's home in Vermont, providing a warm background and texture for the display of their collections. A large lidded jar from La Borne, France, is displayed on a pedestal at the foot of a sunny stairwell.

A Stephen Pearce pottery vase and Simon's Woodbury vase and Charlotte lamp are arranged on a Chinese chest of drawers in a quiet hallway.

OPPOSITE
Simon's Revere hurricanes and a lidded jar by potter Richard Batterham are symmetrically arranged on an antique Irish cupboard.

An assortment of
Simon's and Simon
Pearce glass stemware
is within easy reach
on new, simple pine
shelving in the kitchen.
On the antique English
Tudor chest is a wooden
bowl by Simon and Pia's
son, Andrew Pearce.

OPPOSITE
Safely contained in
an antique Irish wall
cupboard is a collection
of Georgian glass. On
top of the cupboard
is an early American
glass vessel (left) and
on the three-door
cupboard (below)
are a Simon Pearce
Providence centerpiece
and a pottery lamp by
Stephen Pearce.

Pia and Simon's
kitchen table is set
with glassware made
by Simon and Simon
Pearce candlelit
LoveYourBrain bowls,
a Barre pitcher,
and Woodbury
dinner plates.

OPPOSITE
The table and chairs are
by Charles Shackleton.
On the table is glass
made by Simon,
Simon Pearce Silver
Lake tea lights, and
Woodbury dinnerware.
Over the table is a
hanging pendant lamp
by Louis Poulsen,
the lamp that Simon
originally had installed
in his store on Kildare
Street in Dublin.

In the passageway
between the barn frame
structure and another
building of the Pearce
house is a large vessel
by Richard Batterham.

OPPOSITE
Over the fireplace
in the living room
is a painting on
unprimed linen by
Patrick Scott. On
the antique low table
is a free-form glass
Pure Celestial bowl,
designed by Simon
Pearce designers.

On a wall of the Pearce's living room is a wool tapestry by Patrick Scott, woven at Aubusson in France; in front of Scott's work is a 45 Chair by Danish designer Finn Juhl, which Simon's parents had acquired for Kilmahon House in the 1950s.

Placed on the antique Irish sideboard are a bowl by Irish wood turner Keith Mosse and an old, large glass bottle Simon had made into a lamp. On the wall is a painting by Irish artist Jack Yeats, whose work Simon's father, Philip, collected.

OPPOSITE
Simon's free-blown cordial glass pays homage to Georgian stemware.

A portion of Simon's collection of Georgian glass is on display in Pia's study.

OPPOSITE
On a shelf over the fireplace in Pia's study are some of the first pots Simon made under his own name in Ireland in 1967 and the first two glasses he made in London in 1968. On the wall is a painting by Jack Yeats. On the floor is a large vessel by potter Richard Batterham and a steel and wood floor lamp designed by Simon.

In the living room,
a steel floor lamp
designed by Simon
stands next to a 45
Chair by Danish
designer Finn Juhl,
which Simon purchased
to complete a pair with
the original that his
parents had purchased
in the 1950s.

A lamp and a small
covered pot by Miranda
Thomas are composed
with a Richard
Batterham bowl and
a photograph of
Pia and her brother.
The painting is by
Glenn Suokko.

OPPOSITE
As daylight begins
to diminish, Simon's
Hartland hurricane
provides light from a
candle, sheltered from
the wind.

When Simon set up his pottery studio in Ireland in 1967, he made earthenware dinnerware with a white glaze; he retained a collection of it.

In Vermont, he made a set of stemware for his family's use that has not entered into production. Also on the table are Simon's Nantucket hurricane, a recent free-form bowl (holding strawberries), and a Small bowl that he designed in Ireland.

Simon's recent one-of-a-kind free-form glass bowl.

OPPOSITE
A table on an outdoor porch with a bowl by potter Richard Batterham is informally set for drinks with Simon's Essex wine glasses and Norwich beakers.

Simon transported a few large stone-carved vessels from Ireland to Vermont, such as this one used as a planter at the pool house.

OPPOSITE
Simon set a table on a porch with a mix of his glass, pottery, and flatware, as well as work by other designers and makers such as the salt and pepper grinders by Oliver Hemming and soup bowls by Richard Batterham. In the foreground are Simon's Woodbury bowl and wooden cutting and serving bowls by Andrew Pearce.

FOLLOWING SPREAD
Lunch for two is set in the vegetable and cutting garden. The metal settee is Irish Georgian. On the table is pottery by Philip Pearce, glassware Simon made for family use at his Vermont home, and his Revere hurricane and Westport black-handled flatware.

A bowl by Simon, made in the 1980s.

OPPOSITE
On the Pearce's porch table, new hurricanes by Simon Pearce designers are proudly displayed in a row.

THE SIMON PEARCE LIFESTYLE

Early on as a glassmaker, Simon wanted his functional ware to easily fit in a variety of homes and lifestyles. By virtue of the timelessness inherent in his designs, many of his customers in Europe and the United States find ways to integrate his glassware in their own personal fashion. His pieces contentedly reside with a wide range of styles—traditional, classic, contemporary, modern, and casual. When a table is set with Simon's glass—flowers arranged in vases, candles in candleholders lit, bowls filled with food, and wine poured into glasses—an understated elegance emerges. Creating a personal experience with glass is part of the Simon Pearce lifestyle.

Single flower arrangements are very satisfying and do not take away from the beauty of the glass. Simon made a small bud vase in 2014, reminiscent of an old glass milk bottle, as a gift for my wife, Ann.

OPPOSITE
Simon's Low bowl is one of my mother-in-law's favorites. He made it in the 1980s. She keeps it often on a buffet in her dining room throughout the year, where it is quite sculptural, especially when empty. Here, it serves as a centerpiece for floating roses on her back porch.

Simon's Woodbury vase, arranged with purple parrot tulips at Pia's mother's home, is a versatile vessel. Simon has always wanted his vases to be an integral part of the floral display.

OPPOSITE
Simon's Essex red wine glasses and Cavendish goblets and flutes are set on Pia's mother's English gateleg dining table along with her own dinnerware and silverware. She arranged flowering branches, freshly picked from her garden, in a large vase by English potter Richard Batterham.

In a conservatory, Simon's Shelburne vase is arranged with all white flowers. In Pia's mother's house, a dramatic display of delphinium is arranged in a vase designed by Simon Pearce designers.

OPPOSITE
A Pure Middlebury vase, designed by Simon Pearce designers, stands on a stone table in the garden at Pia's mother's house.

FOLLOWING SPREAD
In my home, Simon's Cavendish candlesticks, Woodstock wine glasses, and Thetford tea lights illuminate a dining table set for four with Simon Pearce Cavendish dinnerware.

Also on the table are Simon's Square pitchers and Bud vases and stainless-steel Plata flatware by Georg Jensen.

During one visit we made to Pia's mother's house, she set a festive spring table on her terrace with Simon's Essex stemware and candle globes and her own dinnerware and flatware.

OPPOSITE
A Simon Pearce Woodbury ice bucket doubles as a flower vase for an informal arrangement of fresh-picked tulips.

Simon's penchant for clear glass becomes colorful when something with color is placed inside the glass, such as the Simon Pearce Barre bowl filled with cherries.

OPPOSITE
At my home, we set Simon's free-blown stemware, a Woodbury bowl, and Thetford and Barre tea lights on an outdoor table on our garden terrace with Simon's Westport flatware, a wooden bowl by Andrew Pearce, and Shanagarry Pottery dinnerware made by Simon's brother at Stephen Pearce Pottery in Ireland.

PAGES 112 AND 113
Simon's Woodbury bowl serves as an ice bowl with fresh mint alongside his Woodstock tumblers and Woodstock and Hartland white wine glasses. In the background are his decanters.

PREVIOUS SPREAD
On a table in our family's retreat cabin in the Vermont hills are early examples of Simon's Essex wine glasses and a Woodbury hurricane, a Hartland brandy glass, Ascutney tumblers, and his Woodbury whiskey glasses.

LEFT
We often like to set glass on pottery and find the combination striking, such as Simon's Thetford bowl on his father's Shanagarry Pottery dinner plate. We also find different groupings of glass designs make a table interesting and unique every time we set it.

OPPOSITE
A view of the same table set with Simon's Woodbury hurricane, Hartland white wine glasses, Norwich and Ascutney barware, and Westport flatware.

In our dining room, Simon's Meriden pitcher glows with light from a Thetford tea light.

OPPOSITE
Simon's Nantucket hurricane is the centerpiece for the same table shown with Simon's Bud vases and Simon Pearce Barre goblets and white wine glasses, Barre tea lights, and Belmont dinner plates.

We love candlelight. Simon's Hartland candlesticks are lit on an old French dresser in our kitchen, which keeps our set of Belmont dinnerware close at hand.

OPPOSITE
We often entertain in my studio; it is a nice, large workspace with a fireplace at one end. Illuminated by the glow of fire at a table set for visiting friends are Simon's Essex and Woodstock stemware, Cavendish candlesticks, and Bud vases with Simon Pearce Cavendish dinner plates and pottery bowls by Richard Batterham.

Cavendish candlesticks illuminate an antique Japanese vase filled with bittersweet in the traditional Vermont home of my brother- and sister-in-law. She has a wonderful sense when arranging objects and flowers. He knows a lot about wine.

Simon's Cavendish white wine glasses are filled with a selection from his wine cellar.

OPPOSITE
In the same home, Hartland flutes and Cavendish white wine glasses reside on an old Welsh dresser displayed with two sets of fine Japanese porcelain and an iron teapot by the Japanese designer Suzuki.

An extra-small Revere bowl, used here for serving jam, on Philip Pearce's Shanagarry dinner plate.

OPPOSITE
Simon's Thetford platter is the centerpiece for a Japanese dinner set with a mix of pottery and chopsticks.

SELECTED DESIGNS

Simon has designed and made glass for over forty years, and many of these items remain in production. Today he continues to produce a handful of his earliest designs from his time in Ireland and at his workshops in Vermont and Maryland, and adds new styles annually. Presented here is a selection of fifty objects that Simon and I feel are his most iconic works. Also included are innovative products that designers working at Simon Pearce in recent years have created.

OPPOSITE
Simon created the Large bowl in Ireland and carried the design over to production in Vermont, where it was further developed and renamed the Shelburne bowl.

ESSEX RED WINE

Simon Pearce
Ireland, 1969
(originally named the Round wine)

TRUMPET WINE

Simon Pearce
Ireland, 1975

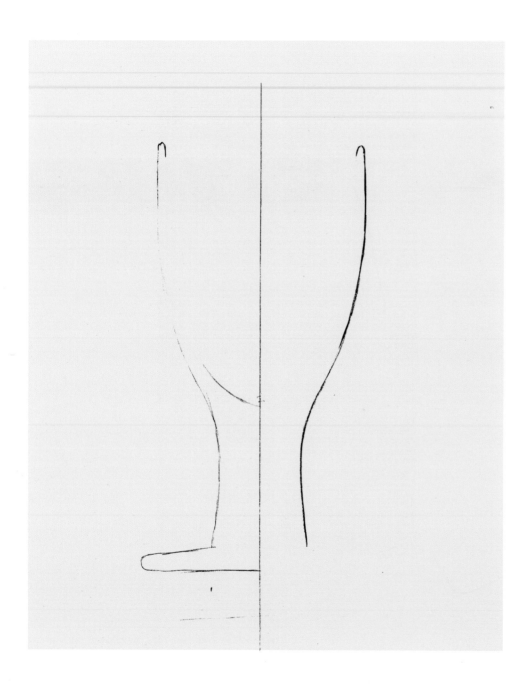

3

CAVENDISH WHITE WINE

Simon Pearce
Ireland, 1976
(originally named the Bell wine)

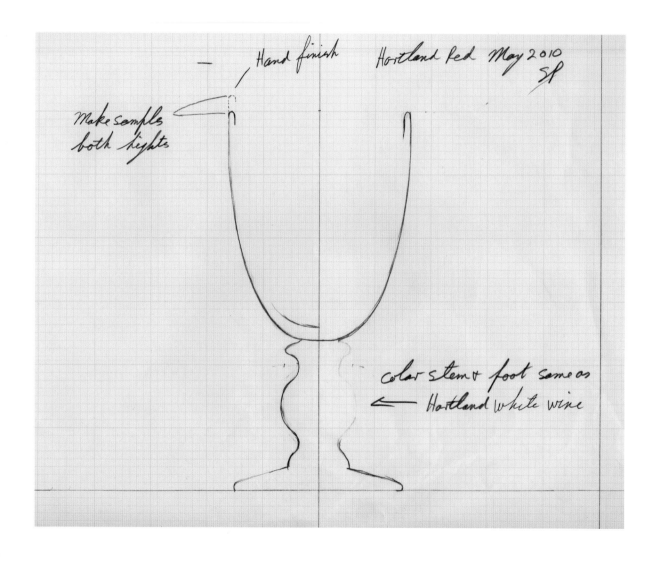

ASCUTNEY WHISKEY

Simon Pearce
Ireland, 1972
(originally named the Whiskey)

7

NORWICH BEAKER

Simon Pearce
Ireland, 1972
(originally named the Beaker)

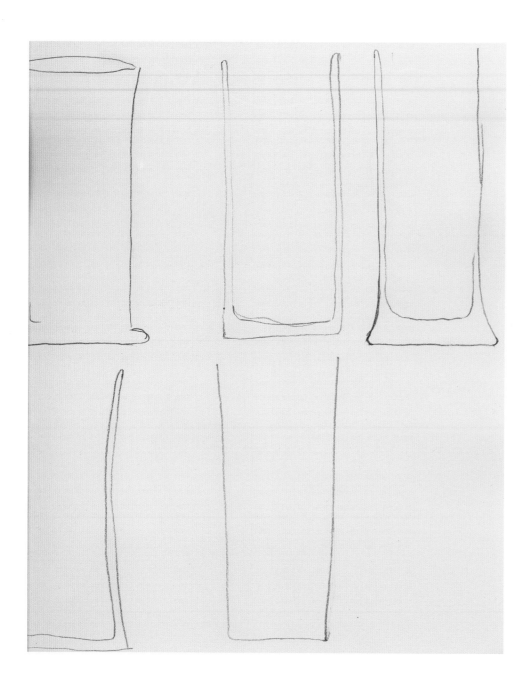

WINDSOR TANKARD

Simon Pearce
Ireland, 1973
(originally named the Tankard)

9

MERIDEN PITCHER

Simon Pearce
Ireland, 1973
(originally named the Round jug)

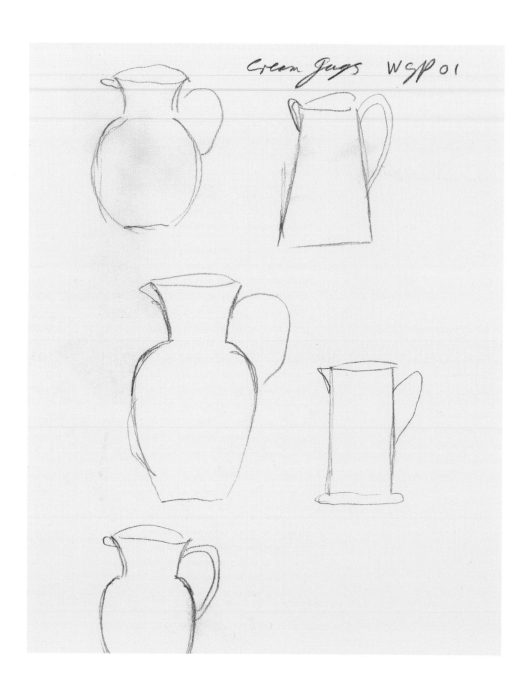

Green Jugs WSP 01

WOODBURY CARAFE

Simon Pearce
Ireland, 1974
(originally named the Square carafe)

II

DECANTER WITH STOPPER

Simon Pearce
Ireland, 1977

WOODBURY PITCHER

Simon Pearce
Vermont, 1993
(originally named the Square pitcher)

ADDISON PITCHER

Simon Pearce designers
Vermont, 2003

MADISON CARAFE

Simon Pearce
Vermont, 2005

ASCUTNEY BEDSIDE CARAFE

Simon Pearce
Vermont, 2006

WELLESLEY CARAFE

Simon Pearce, designed with Pia Pearce
Vermont, 2006

18

BARRE PITCHER

Simon Pearce, designed with Simon
Pearce designers
Vermont, 2007

NORWICH ICE BUCKET

Simon Pearce, designed with Simon
Pearce designers
Vermont, 2001

WOODBURY ICE BUCKET

Simon Pearce designers
Vermont, 2013

22

SHELBURNE BOWL

Simon Pearce
Ireland, 1972
(originally named the Large bowl)

24

WOODBURY BOWL

Simon Pearce
Vermont, 1992
(originally named the Square bowl)

STEM BOWL

Simon Pearce
Vermont, 1995

THETFORD BOWL

Simon Pearce
Vermont, 2001

30

PROVIDENCE CENTERPIECE

Simon Pearce designers
Vermont, 2009

31

PURE MIDDLEBURY BOWL

Simon Pearce designers
Vermont, 2013

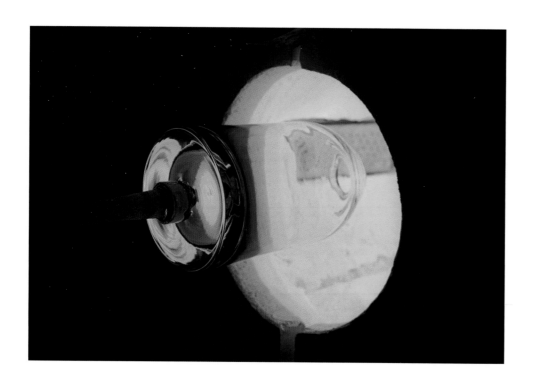

CAVENDISH CANDLESTICK

Simon Pearce
Ireland, 1972
(originally named the Tall candlestick)

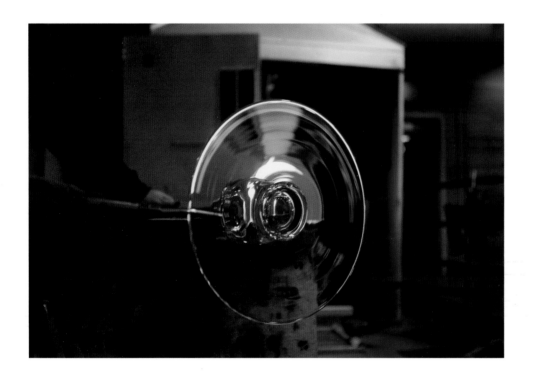

34

HARTLAND HURRICANE

Simon Pearce
Vermont, 1991

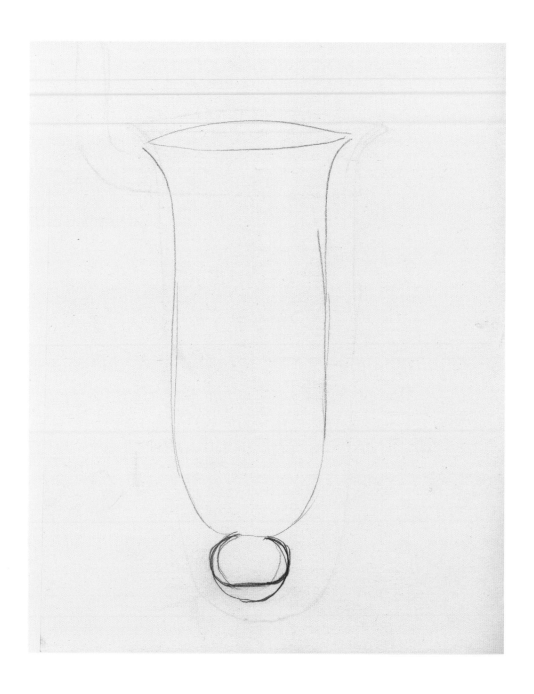

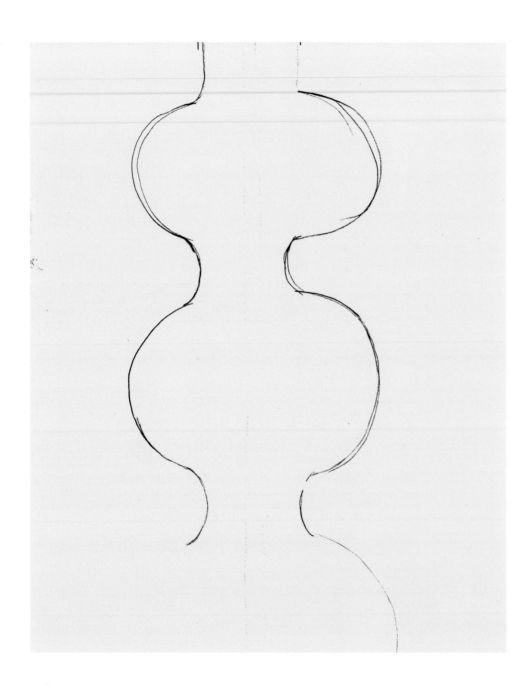

HARTLAND CANDLESTICKS

Simon Pearce
Vermont, 1992

CANDLEHOLDER

Simon Pearce
Vermont, 1995

WOODBURY HURRICANE

Simon Pearce
Vermont, 1998

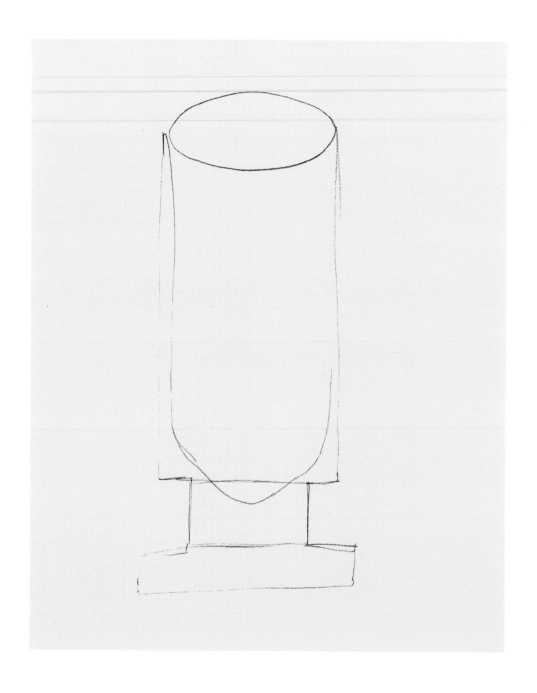

REVERE HURRICANE

Simon Pearce
Vermont, 2002

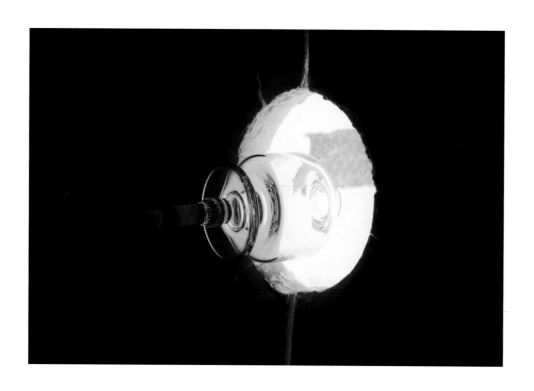

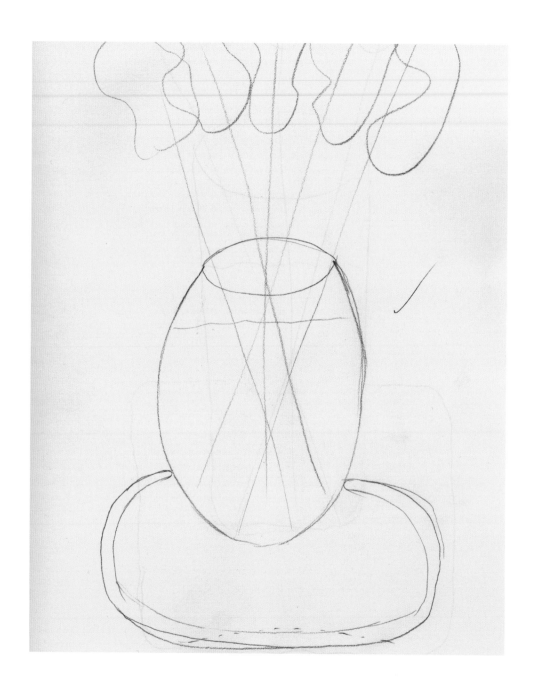

SHELBURNE VASE

Simon Pearce
Ireland, 1974
(originally named the Round vase)

41

WOODBURY VASE

Simon Pearce
Vermont, 1990
(originally named the Square vase)

WESTON VASE

Simon Pearce
Vermont, 2002

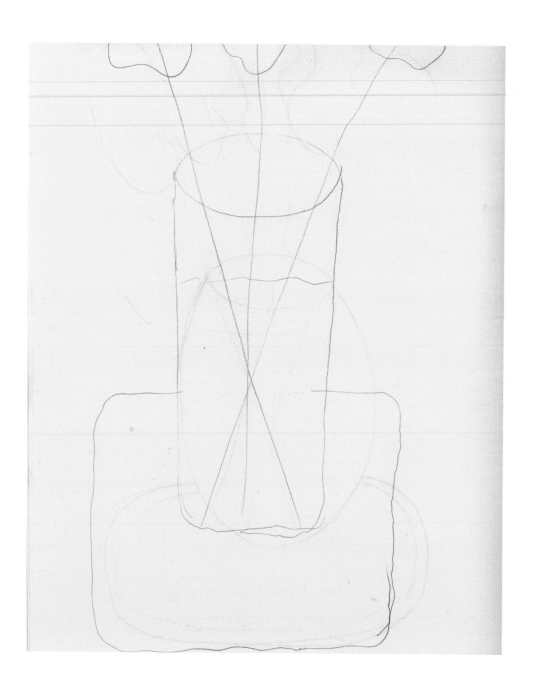

PURE ROUND WRAP VASE

Simon Pearce designers
Vermont, 2013

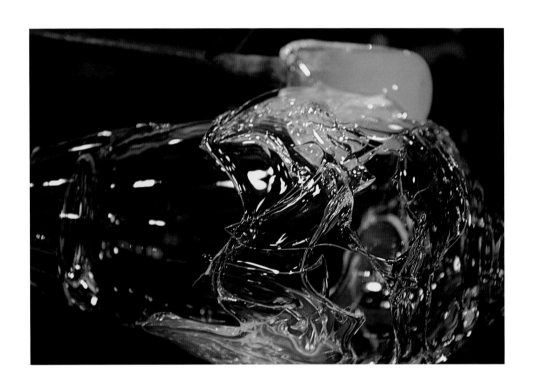

PURE WATER VASE

Simon Pearce designers
Vermont, 2013

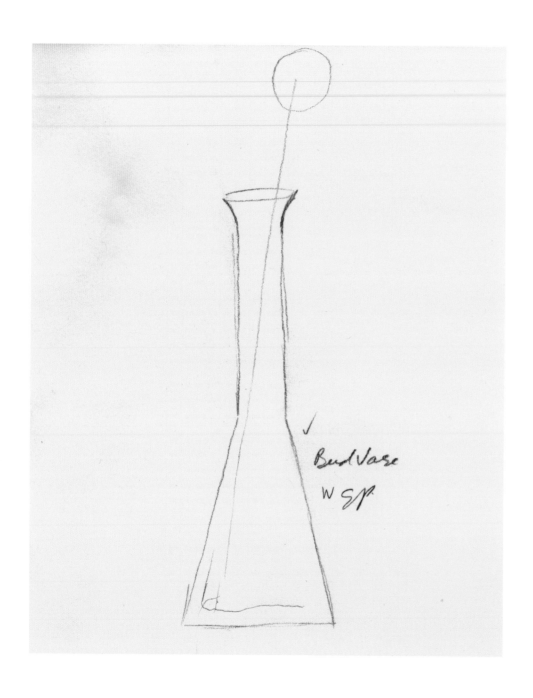

BudVase

W SP

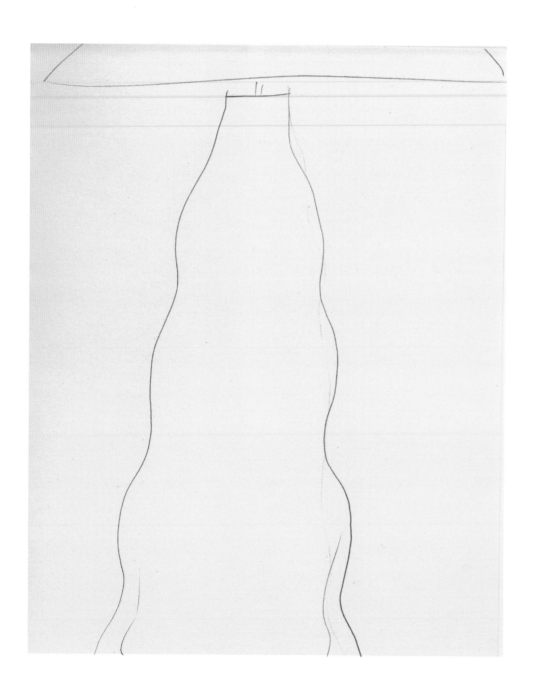

HARTLAND LAMP

Simon Pearce
Vermont, 2003

VERMONT EVERGREEN

Simon Pearce
Vermont, 2006

BELMONT POTTERY

Simon Pearce
Vermont, 1992

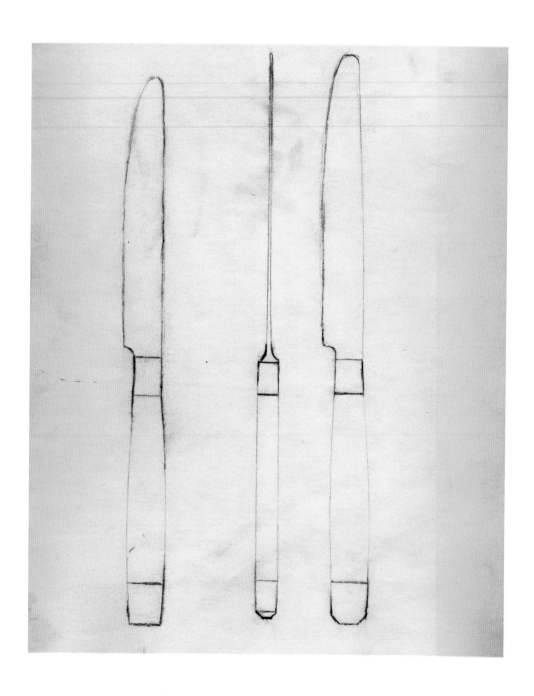

"GOOD DESIGN"
PHILIP PEARCE, POTTERY, AND THE LEACH TRADITION

Simon was initially trained as a potter and knew the craft of making clay pots before he became interested in glass. His parents, Philip and Lucy Pearce, not only schooled him in pottery but also exposed him to good design. Philip was inspired by earlier pottery traditions, and infused his pieces with his modern aesthetic. He demanded quality material from the outset. Philip built a successful pottery business and set an excellent example of high standards for his son, Simon.

During Simon's formative years in Ireland, a studio-pottery renaissance was taking place in Europe, in particular in England. The impact that English potter and teacher Bernard Leach, known as the father of British studio pottery, had on potters is legendary. Leach advocated making one-of-a-kind pieces, but his central tenet of creating beautiful pots for everyday use certainly penetrated the Pearce family philosophy at their pottery in Shanagarry. Many of the studio-potters of Philip Pearce's generation, such as Harry Davis, Michael Cardew, and Lucie Rie, were

Philip Pearce in his study, Kilmahon House, Shanagarry Ireland, 1980s.

Earthenware jug
Nineteenth century
Youghal, County Cork,
Ireland
Collection Simon
Pearce

This type of pot had been made in the same shape, clay composition, and glaze color by generations of Youghal potters.

making pots that captured the attention of artists and artisans. Country potters who made functional ware, such as one of Philip's first instructors, Willie Greene, from Youghal, Ireland, tended to follow the same formal expressions as their cultural and geographical region had dictated for generations. Understanding that utilitarian objects could be attractive with individual character was new. Bernard Leach had brought fresh ideas about pottery to the United Kingdom following his immersion in Japanese culture. In Shanagarry, Ireland, Philip Pearce introduced his sons, Stephen and Simon, to several potters who had been trained by Leach. Simon later observed the same philosophy of functionality and beauty when he decided to make glassware.

Most of the potters whose work Philip admired and collected and that Simon would later expand in his collection were closely interconnected. With the exception of William Staite Murray, Lucie Rie, and Hans Coper, whose work Simon inherited from his father, several of the potters who Simon collected followed the Leach tradition. Simon admires these particular pieces for their beauty and technical execution. Practically all of the pottery he has acquired is made and signed (or stamped) by an individual whom Simon or his father has known. His collection of pottery, as well as glass, furniture, and fine art, are reflective of his discriminating taste. Simon's collection is an homage to creative people.

Philip Pearce knew Bernard Leach, and although he never trained at his pottery, he was inspired by his philosophy; Leach's *A Potter's Book*, published in 1940, was an important practical book for potters who, like Pearce, worked on their own or in small workshops. Although Leach advocated a rather narrow philosophical view of what pottery should be, he also dispelled the mythologies and secrets around technical methods and sought to inspire a new generation of craftspeople by providing them with valuable information and instructions—a "how to" approach to a traditional craft. This highly informative book also explored the strong connections in the cultural relationship between Eastern and Western pottery and advocated that the modern potter seek to make functional ware with individual artistic expression by working "in the same spirit, using the same kind of materials in a straight-forward and natural way."[1] Leach's seminal book has had a lasting influence on potters and, as a significant resource, it continues to inform craftspeople today.

PHILIP PEARCE (1911–1993) had worked as a typographer, printer, and farmer before he developed an interest to become a potter when he was in his early forties. He first trained at Crowan Pottery with Harry and May Davis in Cornwall in 1952. While the

47. Inlaid Porcelain Jar with cut sides by K. Tomimoto. First individual Japanese potter.
48. Cut and planed Stoneware Bowl by the author.
Warm grey and rust glaze.

The cover of Bernard
Leach's seminal
A Potter's Book.

A page from the same
book illustrating works
by Leach's friend,
the potter Tomimoto
Kenkichi, and Leach.

Philip Pearce
Small pitcher
Collection Simon Pearce

Philip Pearce
Bowl
Collection Simon Pearce

OPPOSITE
Philip Pearce
Shanagarry mug,
sauceboat, bowl,
and vase

Pearce family was living at Ballymalloe House, he learned how to make pots from Willie Greene, a master potter and a descendent of one of the oldest pottery families in nearby Youghal. They set up a pottery wheel and work area in one of the greenhouses that Philip had built. Simon was eight years old in 1954 when his parents bought Kilmahon House in Shanagarry and transformed what was formerly a horse stable adjacent to the house into a working pottery. Philip and Lucy Pearce named it Shanagarry Pottery, and opened its doors for business in 1957.

In the early days of the pottery, Philip made pots in the local earthenware tradition, with clay dug from the banks of the Blackwater River valley in Youghal. He began to experiment with different glaze colors and new—more modern—forms. In 1962, Philip developed a design for a simple straight-sided dinner plate, side plate, and mug that was much more contemporary in design than his earlier work. A bold combination of glazes—black on the outside of the forms and white on the inside—were introduced for this new line he called "Shanagarry"; it became an immediate and lasting success.

Unlike the numerous studio potters among his sphere, Philip did not become an artist-potter; he embraced the tenants of traditional production pottery and merged his designs with a dose of modernism to create a successful line of domestic ware. Each year the Pearce family installed their pottery in an exhibition room at Brown Thomas, a high-end department store in Dublin, and each year Philip added to the popular Shanagarry line new designs for bowls, vases, jugs, cups, and more. This annual exhibition became the principal venue where the Pearces sold their pottery. Philip and Lucy were able to build a successful business selling handmade pottery during a period when Ireland was a poor and struggling country.

Through Philip's connections to studio potters in England and his interests and insight into design, the revitalization of pottery in Philip's generation provided Simon with a good model. For Simon, there is a crossover between pottery making and glassblowing; it is the traditional methodology and functionality of both these disciplines that unite them. Because glass is a very different medium than pottery, Simon is not a direct descendent of the Leach tradition, but he is certainly a close cousin to the mainstay of its foundational principles. Where Leach-minded potters looked to ancient Far East pottery for creative inspiration, Simon as a glassmaker was able to look closer to his own roots—to England, Ireland, and the Georgian era—to revitalize glass in his own creative voice.

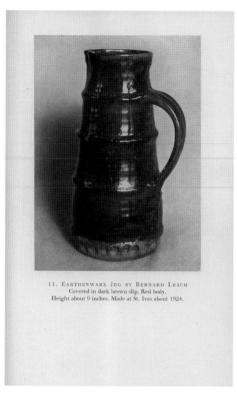

11. EARTHENWARE JUG BY BERNARD LEACH
Covered in dark brown slip. Red body.
Height about 9 inches. Made at St. Ives about 1924.

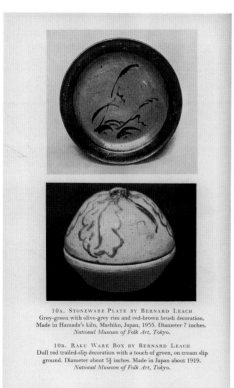

10A. STONEWARE PLATE BY BERNARD LEACH
Grey-green with olive-grey rim and red-brown brush decoration.
Made in Hamada's kiln, Mashiko, Japan, 1955. Diameter 7 inches.
National Museum of Folk Art, Tokyo.

10B. RAKU WARE BOX BY BERNARD LEACH
Dull red trailed-slip decoration with a touch of green, on cream slip
ground. Diameter about 5½ inches. Made in Japan about 1919.
National Museum of Folk Art, Tokyo.

Two pages from Muriel Rose's 1955 book, *Artist-Potters in England*, illustrating work by Bernard Leach.

English potter **BERNARD LEACH** (1887–1979) is considered the father of British studio pottery. Born in Hong Kong, his early background was in art; he studied drawing and painting at the Slade School of Fine Art in London and etching at the London School of Art with the intention of becoming a fine artist. In 1909, when he was twenty-one, he moved to Japan, where his Japanese friend Tomimoto Kenkichi introduced him to pottery. For two years, Leach apprenticed with Ogata Kenzan, one of Japan's most revered potters and the sixth generation in a long line of master potters. Leach's immersion in Eastern philosophy nurtured his life as a potter and developed his artistic vision. Leach made pots in Japan for five years and is said to have been the heir to Kenzan's teachings. In Japan, traditional pottery is highly regarded and equal to poetry and fine art. As a European potter, Leach was able to express the essence of Japanese pottery. Leach was also inspired by Chinese Sung dynasty (960–1279) pottery and most particularly by Korean pottery workshop traditions from the ninth through the fourteenth centuries that were also prevalent in Japan. He was able to draw from ancient methods and invigorate them into a twentieth-century studio practice of the craft.

In 1916, Sōetsu Yanagi, director of the Japan Folk Crafts Museum, enabled Leach to set up a pottery on Yanagi's estate. It was through their friendship that Leach met potter Shoji Hamada in 1919. In 1920, the two potters left Japan for England, where they established the Leach Pottery in St. Ives, Cornwall, England, in the same year. Leach never intended the pottery to be a studio for himself alone: "it was always his intention that it should become, as it did, a place for the exchange of pottery knowledge and for work by a group of craftsmen in conditions that were mutually congenial. He believed in the value to the artist-potter of producing pots for daily household use, in addition to individual more highly-priced pieces. Leach also sought to make the former at a price, which would bring them within the means of all who might wish to buy them. This called for repetition without the loss of quality."[2]

Hamada stayed at St. Ives for three years before returning to Japan permanently, but throughout their lives the two potters remained close friends and important advocates of the studio pottery movement they had worked to create. Leach promoted simple and functional forms and encouraged a blend of Eastern (Korean, Chinese, and Japanese) and Western (English) philosophies and techniques. Noted for his sensitivity in throwing beautiful

Bernard Leach
Pot
Collection Simon Pearce

Harry Davis
Bowl
Collection Simon Pearce

The same bowl,
underside, opposite.

Simon Pearce
Pot with lid
1967

forms and his rich glaze techniques, he is widely respected for his expressive drawing skills, which gives his work its own distinctive character.

Many renowned potters trained at the Leach Pottery and developed their own work motivated by Leach and Hamada's philosophy and teachings. The pottery was an important training ground for the next generation of potters that included Michael Cardew and Harry Davis, followed by another generation including Gwyn Hanssen Pigott and Richard Batterham, all of whom Simon knew or whose work Simon would come to know, respect, and be inspired by.

English potter **HARRY DAVIS** (1910–1986) was born in Cardiff, Wales—the same city where Simon's mother was raised, although the two would not meet one another until many decades later. In the late 1920s, Davis studied pottery at Bournemouth and Poole College of Art and Design in the United Kingdom. He worked in the Poole Pottery in Dorset in the early 1930s before training at the Leach Pottery in Cornwall in 1933, where he developed his skills under the tutelage of Bernard Leach and Leach's potter son, David. His training there formed the foundation of the style he was to employ throughout his long career.

In 1937, Davis left the Leach Pottery for Ghana, Africa, where he taught art and pottery at the English-run Achimota College until he suggested that Michael Cardew succeed him in 1942. In 1938, he had married May Davis (1914–1995), also a talented potter, whom he had met during his training at St. Ives. After World War II, in 1946, the Davises established the Crowan Pottery in Cornwall, where they produced utilitarian domestic ware. Philip Pearce trained with Davis in Cornwall in 1952. Harry and May Davis moved to Nelson, New Zealand, in 1962 and set up Crewenna Pottery, a studio to develop their own work as well as a school to train potters. When Simon was sixteen, he began his apprenticeship with the Davises at Crewenna and worked there for two years.

Early in his career Davis was influenced by Leach's philosophy, but he had an independent spirit and went on to form his own belief that challenged the pure artist-potter leanings advocated by Leach in favor of a more ascetic, practical side of pottery. Davis authored *The Potter's Alternative*, a book that focused on the materials and tools of the craft, rather than Eastern philosophy and the studio-pottery movement that was prevalent in books such as Leach's *A Potter's Book*. "The nature of pots as receptacles, and the need for such things in everyone's daily life, has always made the potter a valuable member of the community. This is the

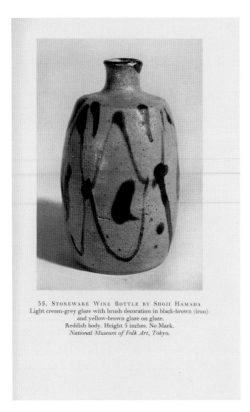

55. STONEWARE WINE BOTTLE BY SHOJI HAMADA
Light cream-grey glaze with brush decoration in black-brown (iron) and yellow-brown glaze on glaze.
Reddish body. Height 5 inches. No Mark.
National Museum of Folk Art, Tokyo.

B. STONEWARE BOTTLE BY SHOJI HAMADA. 1935
Tenmoku glaze with wax-reserve brush decoration.
Height 14 inches. No Mark.
Walker Art Gallery, Liverpool. See page 15

Two pages from Muriel Rose's 1955 book, *Artist-Potters in England*, illustrating work by Shoji Hamada.

basic practical side of the potter's role. . . . The term 'artist' never entered the vocabulary of many generations of potters prior to the industrial revolution, but they were artists in the best sense—the unselfconscious sense."[3]

Davis's pots are humble in shape and traditional in form. He was famously known as a strong and prolific thrower. Using glazes in natural, earthy colors—brown, gold, black, and red ochre—he decorated his domestic wares with bold unrepresentative brushwork, much of which related to nature.

Simon's training at Crewenna was successful; he gained skill and confidence in throwing pots. His plan was to move back to Shanagarry to help his father and brother at the family pottery. When Simon finished his pottery apprenticeship in New Zealand in 1965, he met up with his brother, Stephen, who was living in Japan, and they made an extensive tour of Japan and continental Asia. They first visited Shoji Hamada at his pottery in Mashiko, Japan, where Simon purchased a few of the potter's decorated incense boxes in 1966 (see opposite).

Japanese potter **SHOJI HAMADA** (1894–1978) was a member of the *mingei* movement—a term crafted by its founder Sōetsu Yanagi (1889–1961) that connotes a modern return to Japanese traditional folk art. *Mingei* artists and craftspeople looked to anonymous utilitarian crafts, and in particular pottery, from the Edo (1603–1868) and Meiji (1868–1912) periods for creative inspiration.

Through an introduction from Yanagi, Hamada met English potter Bernard Leach in Japan in 1919. Hamada, a student at the time, was impressed by Leach's work, which he had seen in an exhibition—and he and Leach quickly developed a spiritual kinship through their work. In 1920, the two potters left Japan for St. Ives, Cornwall, England, to establish the Leach Pottery. Leach, together with Hamada, changed the English artist-potter's whole approach to his or her craft.[4] Their philosophy, which promoted a blend of Eastern and English pottery traditions, was immediately widespread and continued to influence potters throughout the twentieth century. Their influence is still felt in the twenty-first century. Shoji Hamada's exhibitions in London excited his fellow potters and, both by the impact of his work and his personality, he may be said to have had an influence equal to that of Leach or Staite Murray.[5] Hamada spent a few years at the Leach Pottery before returning to Japan in 1924, where he remained at the forefront of ceramics ideology and pottery making his entire life.

Hamada looked to ancient Japanese folk pottery traditions from the previous four centuries, drew on these inspirations, and translated them into his own visual, expressive language. His pots

Shoji Hamada
Incense box
1960s
Collection Simon Pearce

William Staite Murray
Bowl
Collection Simon Pearce

William Staite Murray
Bowl
Collection Simon Pearce

OPPOSITE
William Staite Murray
Pot
Collection Simon Pearce

combine to an unusual degree rough, apparent casualness with extreme subtlety both in form and color. His brushwork can rise to a lyric sensibility and has a notable strength and freedom—the heritage from generations for whom the brush has been the accepted tool for writing and drawing.[6] Through his prodigious output of ceramic jars, vases, teapots, tea bowls, and brush pots, the impact Hamada had on pottery as a modern craft was profound in his own country and in England and the United States. Regarded as one of the most important potters of the twentieth century, Hamada's work is widely collected. In 1955, he was honored as a Living National Treasure, one of the highest accolades bestowed in Japan.

Philip Pearce knew potter **WILLIAM STAITE MURRAY** (1881–1962) when they both lived in London, and he purchased several pieces from Murray's gallery shows, many of which Simon later inherited. Murray was born in London when Queen Victoria ruled the United Kingdom of Great Britain and Ireland. When Murray began his pottery career, he did not know Leach and worked independently of the Leach tradition. After studying pottery at the Camberwell School of Arts and Crafts in London from 1909 to 1912, and working at the Omega Workshop with Bloomsbury group members Duncan Grant and Vanessa Bell, Murray established his own pottery in Rotherhithe, London. In the early 1920s, England was becoming a hotbed of studio pottery, and Murray, having seen an exhibition of Shoji Hamada's work in London formed a friendship with him, when Hamada was in England setting up the Leach Pottery in Cornwall.

Murray's work took a turn and his pots began to be acknowledged for their technical quality, glazing, and decoration. His pottery soon claimed attention and was exhibited alongside paintings by the livelier of the young artists of the day—Ben Nicholson, Christopher Wood, Frances Hodgkins, and others. This was significant, for Murray aspired to gain acceptance for pottery as a medium comparable to painting or sculpture.[7] His stoneware pots became highly collectible and he became financially successful, an accomplishment not generally afforded to many active potters at the time. In 1925, he was appointed head of the Pottery Department at the Royal College of Art in London. He built a studio in Kent, followed by another pottery in Berkshire, and was keenly interested in the quality of kilns and of building his own, going as far as patenting his kiln design.

Unlike his contemporaries—many of who were devoted followers of Bernard Leach—Murray scorned utility in his own work and equated his pot making with fine art endeavors. "He

reduction fires his pots to stoneware temperature and adopted an aesthetic based on Zen Buddhism and Eastern philosophy, believing that pottery was a fine art form along with sculpture and painting."[8] He adopted the fine art practice of giving some of his pots titles, as a painter would give canvases.

English potter MICHAEL CARDEW (1901–1983) is regarded among the finest potters of the twentieth century, and is reputed to be one of the best slipware potters. Cardew was one of the first generation of potters to apprentice under Bernard Leach and Shoji Hamada at the Leach Pottery in England in 1923. When he was twenty-five, he restored the rundown Winchcombe Pottery in Gloucestershire and sought to revive old English slipware methods to make affordable pottery for a wide audience. Cardew achieved success with his slipware production and kept the pottery going until 1939, when he left it to potter Alfred Raymond (Ray) Finch to run while he set up his new pottery at Wenford Bridge in Cornwall. Cardew moved to Ghana, Africa, where he succeeded Harry Davis as head of the Art Department at the English-run Achimota College from 1942 to 1948, and in Abuja, Nigeria, from 1951 to 1965, to teach pottery to African students and to further his own work. However, he returned to England and spent most of his life in Cornwall at his Wenford Bridge Pottery to produce his own earthenware and stoneware pottery and to teach students.

Cardew disdained the romanticizing of the past and of Japanese pottery that Leach and many of his followers had valued and chose to infuse his pots with his own Cornish heritage and its pottery traditions. His pots are bold and often roughly shaped, and the decorations are fluid. There is a directness and spontaneity to them that reveals Cardew's confidence and individuality. He also believed in a spiritualty associated with pottery making. Cardew came to believe that potters should make everything they worked with, or their pots would not be fully alive. They should dig the raw materials for their own clays and glazes, and make their own bricks for their kilns, and cut their own firewood.[9]

Simon's brother, Stephen, trained with Cardew at Wenford Bridge Pottery from 1963 to 1964, and when Simon visited his brother at Wenford he purchased several of Cardew's pieces. Miranda Thomas, who would later work for Simon and whose work Simon collects, apprenticed with and worked for Cardew from 1979 to 1980. Cardew wrote two important books, *Pioneer Pottery* (1969) and *A Pioneer Potter* (1988), and, like Leach's *A Potter's Book*, Cardew's books have become important technical and inspiring resources for potters.

Michael Cardew
Bowl
1960s
Collection Simon Pearce

Michael Cardew
Bowl
1960s
Collection Simon Pearce

OPPOSITE
Michael Cardew
Vessel with lid
1960s
Collection Simon Pearce

Lucie Rie
Cup
Collection Simon Pearce

Lucie Rie
Sauceboat
Collection Simon Pearce

Lucie Rie
Sauceboat
Collection Simon Pearce

OPPOSITE
Lucie Rie
Bowl
Collection Simon Pearce

Although Philip Pearce's sensibilities first leaned toward the Leach tradition, he could also see quality and excellence in other ceramic expressions. Austrian-born **LUCIE RIE** (1902–1995) was a highly successful potter who first lived in Vienna and trained at that city's progressive Kunstgewerbeschule. She also studied with the architect and designer Josef Hoffmann and was influenced by his teachings, which advocated the development of a new Austrian style in architecture and industrial design, an aesthetic and lifestyle that was quintessentially modern and urban. When Rie became established, she showed her pots to wealthy collectors in her apartment, which had been designed in 1929 by Ernst Plischke. She became well known in Vienna and her work was highly respected by her contemporaries and sought after by collectors. Through her oeuvre, Rie achieved critical acclaim and financial success. However, to escape Nazi persecution she was forced to leave Vienna before the onset of World War II and moved to London, where she lived the rest of her life.

In 1939, Rie established a pottery at Albion Mews, near Hyde Park, London. Rie enlisted Plischke to again help her with the design of her living quarters. She had arranged for her modern apartment in Vienna to be carefully dismantled, transported to London, and reinstalled on the second floor above the pottery. During Rie's years in England, unlike many of her British contemporaries who were followers of Bernard Leach and produced down-to-earth functional ware, Rie chose to develop her craft in her own way—a style that was decidedly modern. She mostly made pots to be displayed, not for the pantry or to be used in the oven and rarely at the table. In Britain, Leach was generally regarded as the official spokesman for studio pottery as well as for the wider craft movement, which was underpinned by an almost moral commitment to handwork. Much of the work was intended to be useful, either symbolically or practically, and committed to the concept of "standards" in which pots could embody "values." Such concepts had little meaning for Rie.[10] Rie and Leach developed a deep professional relationship and long lasting freindship; however, Leach was fiercely critical of Rie's work, not understanding nor appreciating its delicate forms and modern expression; it was not at all like the earthy Eastern-inspired or English work he championed.

Philip Pearce knew Rie from London and bought some of her pottery. Simon grew to appreciate Rie's work in his childhood home in Shanagarry, where it was artfully placed—not used at the table. Rie, well known for her one-of-a-kind pieces, also produced some functional objects. Simon responded foremost to

Hans Coper
Pot
Collection Simon Pearce

OPPOSITE
Hans Coper
Pot
Collection Simon Pearce

these particular pieces. There is a simplicity and directness to her pots—the delicate, natural forms and the textured glazes are captivating. Simon admires what he calls "a lovely deepness in the glazes—'richness' is the word—very sophisticated and simple." In the 1950s, Rie created a few sets of utilitarian vessels—cups, coffee-pots, pitchers—in stoneware and glazed them in a bold combination of black and white. One set is in the collection of the Victoria and Albert Museum in London and another at the Sainsbury Centre for Visual Arts in Norwich, England. Rie's pottery had one of the marked influences for Philip's design and black-and-white glazes of his highly successful Shanagarry range. Her work also made an impact on Simon due to its modern simplicity.

Rie's work was widely exhibited at museums during her lifetime. In 1994, a year before Rie's death, the Metropolitan Museum of Art in New York held a major show of her work, which also included pieces by her colleague and friend, potter Hans Coper.

German born **HANS COPER** (1920–1981) left Germany to escape Nazi oppression and lived his adult life in England, where in 1946, he began working as an assistant to Lucie Rie. While at Rie's Albion Mews pottery studio in London, he worked alongside her for ten years and learned the craft of producing vessels. In 1958, Coper established his own studio in Hertfordshire and quickly became known throughout the studio-pottery movement.

Philip Pearce knew Hans Coper. He attended his gallery shows in London and purchased several pieces, and Simon eventually inherited many of them. Coper's works are among the examples of pottery in Simon's collection that are intentionally pure artistic expressions instead of utilitarian. Coper is considered an artist-potter; his distinctive sculptural stoneware pots were intended as unique works of ceramic art. His style was independent of any school or tradition; he was not a follower of Murray, Leach, or Hamada and his work does not exhibit any noticeable Eastern influence. Lucie Rie was his teacher and mentor, but Coper was an original. His geometric vessel forms are dignified, and his sparing use of glazes is usually limited to a palette of earth tones. The surfaces are often textured and decorated with scratched or incised marks or lines.

Coper taught ceramics at the Royal College of Art in London in the 1960s and is highly regarded in the pottery field as a principal artistic leader. During his lifetime, his pots were widely exhibited in galleries—often alongside pots by Lucie Rie—and sought after by collectors. His work can be seen today in major museum collections such as the Victoria and Albert Museum in London and the Metropolitan Museum of Art in New York.

Tapio Wirkkala
Ovalis vase
1958
Glass
Collection Ann and
Glenn Suokko

Georg Jensen
Plata flatware
1950s
Stainless-steel
Collection Ann and
Glenn Suokko

Charles Eames
Molded plywood
dining chair
1953
Plywood and steel
Collection Ann and
Glenn Suokko

"DESIGN IN IRELAND"

When Philip and Lucy Pearce traveled to Scandinavia in the 1950s, Scandinavian design was capturing attention all over Europe. It was the place to go if one wanted to see or buy well-designed, contemporary household goods and furniture. During their trips, they purchased chairs by Danish designer Finn Juhl, cookware by Arabia, and Georg Jensen's Plata stainless-steel flatware, and stainless-steel pots and pans by Alfa Laval. The Pearces were creative in their approach to integrating contemporary design with traditional Irish crafts as well as with their more elegant furnishings from the English and Irish Georgian era.

In the 1950s, the vibrant design culture in Scandinavia shook the design and lifestyle markets in Europe and the United States. Scandinavian designed products were exported and sold in many parts of the world, including work by leading designers such as Alvar Aalto (furniture and glass), Kaj Franck (glass and tableware), Maija Isola (Marimekko fabrics), Tapio Wirkkala (glassware), Arne Jacobsen (furniture), and Hans J. Wegner (furniture), and by companies such as Electrolux (household appliances), Ikea (home furnishings), Orrefors (glassware), and Bang & Olufsen (electronics). Each year from 1951 until 1970 exceptional Scandinavian designers were recognized with the prestigious Lunning Prize, which helped create a Scandinavian design culture and recognized designers from Denmark, Sweden, Norway, and Finland as among the leading innovators and tastemakers in the world.

In the United States, design was also a hotbed of innovation and new creative expression, with designers who had studied or taught at the legendary Cranbrook Academy of Art in Michigan at the forefront, such as Eero Saarinen (architecture and furniture), Charles Eames (furniture), Harry Bertoia (furniture), Florence Knoll (furniture), Marianne Strengell (textiles), and Jack Lenor Larsen (textiles). Cranbrook design penetrated American culture; it was quick to reach the design elite as well as the middle class from coast to coast.

Design is the expression of the spirit of the time. In the 1950s in Scandinavia and the United States, design had become a critical cultural agenda and a major new industry in a growing competitive commercial environment. In all design disciplines—architecture, furniture, tableware, textiles, glass—many Scandinavian and American designers excelled at reimagining the notions of consumer home products and interior design. Ironically, based on Shoji Hamada's visit to Charles Eames in Los Angeles in 1954, Hamada and Leach, the two prevailing intellectual leaders of

Lucy and Philip Pearce, 1957,
Ballycotton Bay, Ireland.

the handcraft movement, agreed that design needed to evolve in order for traditions and handcraftsmanship to remain vital in a new contemporary scientific and industrial world, Leach writing, "That we need a new kind of designer has been demonstrated by Danish architects; that creative design of mechanical reproduction requires fresh, free, leadership is shown by Eames and his like."[11]

Ireland in the 1950s was culturally rich but creatively had remained isolated. Innovation and modern design had not yet reached Ireland. Well informed and curious, Philip and Lucy Pearce were aware of the excitement around new design in other countries of the world. Unlike other potters in rural Ireland who continued to produce traditional pots, Philip was eager to embrace modernism. He began to experiment with new simplified forms and glaze techniques and introduced some successful designs to his customers. At the same time, the Irish government realized that design in Ireland was lagging behind the thirst for contemporary quality design so they invited five experts from the Scandinavian Design Group—Kaj Franck, Erik Herløw, Åke Huldt, Gunnar Biilmann Petersen, and Erik Chr. Sørenesen—to come to Ireland to make an assessment of the state of design and to offer advice. The team of Scandinavians toured all over Ireland to study the various design, home furnishings, and product industries, and in 1961 they compiled their findings in a book entitled *Design in Ireland*. Philip Pearce's pottery was among the few designs in Ireland that received acknowledgment—it was held up as an example of good design and this was certainly a great tribute to Philip Pearce and his wife, Lucy.

A NEW GENERATION

Philip Pearce
Cup
1950s
Collection Simon Pearce

Philip and Lucy Pearce brought a strong sense and a love of good design to Kilmahon House. They did not adhere to any one particular focus or time period, but quality always remained at the core of their purchases. Simon's love of design was cultivated by their example. His taste for traditional crafts opened up to fresh ideas and to work by a new generation of potters and artists.

In Simon's pottery collection, Arabia's egg cup is a good example of pure modern design. Made of porcelain, its gentle curves, simple white glaze, and intended use appeal to Simon's love of form and function. It is multipurpose; it can be used as a holder for a soft-boiled egg in its shell and, when turned upside down, as a bowl for an egg out of its shell.

In 1873, Rörstrand, a Swedish company, set up its pottery factory, **ARABIA**, in Finland, with a plan to easily export its goods

Arabia
Egg cup
1950s
Collection Simon Pearce

Gwyn Hanssen Pigott
Lidded pot
Collection Simon Pearce

Gwyn Hanssen Pigott
Bowl
Collection Simon Pearce

OPPOSITE
Gwyn Hanssen Pigott
Bowl
Collection Simon Pearce

to nearby Russia, which had vast market potential. In a short time, the Arabia factory was also producing much of Finland's pottery and ceramic ware. The factory changed ownership and became a Finnish company in the early 1900s. Today, Arabia is sold worldwide and is one of Finland's best-known producers of pottery and tableware. The design-centric company has a history of staying a step ahead of current trends and lifestyles. In Finland, Arabia, like textile company Marimekko, is considered a hallmark of Finnish design.

GWYN HANSSEN PIGOTT (1935–2013) was Australia's most illustrious potter, known for her clean, crisp, and modern style. She studied pottery at the University of Melbourne, graduating in 1954. She trained with Australian potter Ivan McMeekin— who had apprenticed with Bernard Leach and Michael Cardew in England—at his Sturt Pottery in New South Wales, in southeastern Australia, from 1955 to 1957. Inspired by Leach and the studio-pottery movement in Great Britain, she moved to England in 1958, where she worked with Ray Finch at Winchcombe Pottery and in the same year apprenticed under Bernard Leach and later trained with Michael Cardew. She took classes with Lucie Rie at the Camberwell School of Arts and Crafts in London. It was most likely Rie that inspired in the young potter a sense of modernism and artistry in her domestic ware.

In 1960, she established her first studio in Notting Hill, London. Six years later she moved with her husband, Louis Hanssen, to France and set up a pottery in the Loire Valley to develop her work further until 1973, when she returned to Australia with her second husband, John Pigott, to establish her pottery studio in Tasmania in 1974.

Hanssen Pigott's interest in ancient Chinese pottery is clearly evident in her work. Revered for her throwing technique, gentle forms, use of raw materials, and Sung dynasty–inspired muted glazes, her elegant smooth-surfaced stoneware and porcelain pots are often not decorated. Later in her career, she transcended the craft of pottery making to sculptural expression in ceramics. She developed a new artistic direction by taking her simple domestic ware and assembling several of them into carefully considered compositions, drawing parallels to the spirit of still-life paintings of Georgio Morandi. Her work is in private collections and prestigious museums, among them the Australian National Gallery, Victoria and Albert Museum, and Los Angeles County Museum of Art.

When he was traveling in France in the early 1970s, Simon visited Gwyn Hanssen Pigott and her pottery in the village of

La Borne pot
Collection Simon Pearce

La Borne pot
Collection Simon Pearce

Richard Batterham
Faceted bowl
1990s
Collection Simon Pearce

OPPOSITE
Richard Batterham
Large vessel
1990s
Collection Simon Pearce

LA BORNE in the Loire Valley. La Borne is famous for its sand-stone clay—a consistency so perfect it can be dug from the ground and used without additional processing to make highly durable stoneware pots. Simon purchased some of Hanssen Pigott's pots as well as several La Borne pots—large lidded storage jars and olive oil jars. The traditional storage pots of the region were often unglazed and wood fired, creating a random "flashing" effect with uneven natural coloration. Similar rustic vessels continue to be made in La Borne, and still with great skill, owing to the apprenticeship process that has been historically important to the La Borne potters. The La Borne vessels are certainly not pots made by studio- or artist-potters but are works by well-trained potters in production potteries. Although made by an individual, the pots possess a strong degree of anonymity as well as rustic charm and they appeal to Simon's sense of simplicity and integrity of form, materials, and function.

Regarded as one of the finest living British potters, RICHARD BATTERHAM (1936–) trained under the English potter Donald Potter, and he studied at the Leach Pottery in St. Ives. Batterham's work is faithful to the Leach philosophy but he went on to develop his own distinctive style.

In 1959, Batterham established his pottery in Durweston, Dorset, where he built his own kilns to produce a range of traditional domestic stoneware with understated wood ash glazes as well as some vessels that were inspired by—and suggestive of—ancient Khmer (now Cambodia) and Korean pottery that was prevalent from the ninth through the fourteenth centuries. Leach and Hamada had also created one-of-a-kind pots reminiscent of this genre. Batterham's limited repertory of distinctive vessels—vases, bowls, bottles, and lidded jars—bear the spirit of ancient works in form, detailing, glaze, and minimal decoration, but he brings to his expression a facility of the craft and a wisdom of individuality that is rare today. His keen historical insight combined with his skill in throwing forms and sensitive glazing techniques are unsurpassed. Batterham brings a similar level of intelligence and skill in his unique pieces to his functional ware.

Working independently and keeping production decidedly small and focused, Batterham, like Shoji Hamada, chooses to not mark his work with a potter's seal. Nevertheless, for those who know his pottery, it is unmistakably recognizable and highly regarded. Simon knew of and admired Batterham's work first through designer David Mellor, whose store in Sloane Square in London sold Batterham's pottery and Simon's glass. Over many years, Simon has acquired several of the potter's one-of-a-kind

pieces as well as many examples of his functional ware—soup bowls, cups, serving bowls—that he and his family use every day.

Simon's older brother, **STEPHEN PEARCE** (1943–), worked as a young teenager alongside Simon in the family's Shanagarry Pottery and later trained in England with potter Ray Finch at Winchcombe Pottery in Gloucestershire, and with Michael Cardew at Wenford Bridge Pottery in Cornwall, to learn how to make functional ware. He also studied in France and then moved to Japan for two years to work with potter Kaneshige Toyo, who during his life had been one of Japan's National Living Treasures.

Like his father and brother, Stephen is also interested in producing utilitarian objects for everyday use and offering them to a wide audience. In 1973, Stephen built his own house and pottery on the Pearce family property at Shanagarry. Under the name Stephen Pearce Pottery, he produces a distinctive line of hand-decorated terra-cotta earthenware with clay dug from the local Blackwater River valley in Youghal. In 1993, Stephen took over Shanagarry Pottery. Kilmahon House and the pottery were sold in 2004. In addition to his own pottery, Stephen continues to produce Shanagarry Pottery's well-known earthenware range with its bold, distinctive black-and-white glaze.

American **MIRANDA THOMAS** (1959–) studied pottery in England at the West Surrey College of Art and Design. From 1979 to 1980, she apprenticed and worked for Michael Cardew at his Wenford Bridge Pottery in Cornwall, England. Thomas is also a potter who bridges the gap between studio pottery and production pottery. As a student, she was inspired by the Leach pottery tradition as well as the writings of Japanese pottery scholar and *mingei* movement founder Sōetsu Yanagi. Thomas's artistic interest in patterns and symbolism is drawn from ancient Chinese, Japanese, Islamic, and Australian aboriginal traditions (she lived in Australia as a teenager).

When Simon established his glassblowing workshop in Quechee, Vermont, he was looking for a potter to create a pottery at his mill and offered the job to Thomas. In 1983, she moved to Vermont, trained a team of talented potters to work with her at Simon Pearce, and over a few years increased its pottery production to become a viable business. Thomas left Simon Pearce in 1988 to start her own studio at her home, later expanding and moving it to a building adjacent to the mill in Bridgewater, Vermont, where her husband, Charles Shackleton, had created a furniture-making workshop. In 2000, the couple combined their businesses into ShackletonThomas and opened a store under their new name at the Bridgewater mill.

Simon Pearce
Small bowl
1970s

By the late 1970s, Simon had shifted away from traditional forms and focused on simplified shapes that had more mass and thickness to the glass, edging closer to a contemporary style.

Simon Pearce
Ashtray
1970s

OPPOSITE
Stephen Pearce
Vase
2013
Collection Simon Pearce

Thomas's pottery is recognized for its decorative drawing and carved surfaces. She produces large-scale individual pieces for art gallery exhibitions and has been commissioned to create diplomatic gifts and commemorations. However, her primary business is to make functional pottery—plates, bowls, vases, and mugs—and offer them to a broad market that appreciates utilitarian objects made by hand.

In Simon's collection of crafts, Thomas is the youngest in the intricate circle of potters and mentors closely tied to the Leach legacy and its subsequent protégés. Just as many of these potters, including Thomas, have trained other potters to learn the pottery craft, the glassblowing trade has also historically preserved an apprenticeship tradition, whereby a master glassblower trains a beginner glassblower in the art of making glass. Working closely with a master glassblower, an apprentice glassblower often takes three to six years to gain the knowledge, strength, and skill to make most of the pieces in the Simon Pearce glassware repertory. Several glassblowers have stayed with Simon Pearce for many years; others have gone on to pursue their own careers in glass or other fields.

CHARLES SHACKLETON (1958–) started his creative work life as a glassblower, training with Simon Pearce in Bennettsbridge at the transitional moment when Simon was moving his glassblowing business to Vermont. Shackleton followed Simon to work with him at his workshop in Quechee, Vermont, in 1981. But after several years, Shackleton's interest in blowing glass shifted to an aspiration of making furniture.

Shackleton grew up near Dublin, Ireland, where he was surrounded by classic Georgian architecture and furniture. He often spent summers in the countryside and at the seashore in Ireland's western counties. He studied at the West Surrey College of Art and Design in England. Today he lives high in the Vermont hills in a nineteenth-century "Cape"-style cottage, full of handmade furniture, pottery, artwork, and crafts. His furniture workshop and store in Bridgewater are not far from his home—just a few miles, all down a long stonewall-lined "dirt" road. In his work, as in his life, he blends cultures that are deeply rooted in his creative spirit: Ireland, where he was born and raised; England, where he went to school; and Vermont, where he has created a life of making things with his wife and potter Miranda Thomas.

His furniture designs are his interpretation of a mix of Irish Georgian and country furniture. It is the lasting quality and timeless appeal of the classic style of Ireland's Georgian design renaissance and the rustic, simpler sensibilities of Ireland's rural

Miranda Thomas
Beaker
1990s
Collection Simon Pearce

OPPOSITE
Charles Shackleton
Pedestal dining table
1990s
Collection Simon Pearce

Andrew Pearce
Champlain bowl
2015
Collection Simon Pearce

OPPOSITE
Andrew Pearce
Live Edge bowl
2015
Collection Simon Pearce

heritage mixed with an American sense of scale that find their way into Shackleton's furniture. Classic simplicity and symmetry are indicative of his work.

As with much of the pottery and artwork that Simon chooses to live with or collect, Shackleton's furniture designs possess references to the past and reflect modern individual character and fine quality execution.

Simon left the family pottery business by 1970 and a decade later left Ireland to start his own glass business in Vermont. Following the family tradition, **ANDREW PEARCE** (1981–), having worked at Simon Pearce for ten years learning just about everything there is to know about making glass, decided to branch out on his own. His entrepreneurial spirit and appreciation of wood as a material determined his career path. He studied with woodworker JoHannes Michelsen, in Manchester, Vermont, and discovered his passion for turning wood on a lathe, which ultimately led him to make wooden bowls. In 2015, he opened a workshop and store in Hartland, Vermont, just a few miles from his father's enterprise in Quechee, Vermont.

Andrew approaches making things by hand in a resourceful way; technical innovation is part of the process. Based on an old Vermont machine he discovered while researching wood manufacturing, he designed and built equipment and machinery that allows little waste. Rather than make one bowl out of a chunk of wood, he devised a system to make two or three bowls from the same amount of wood, by carefully cutting each bowl under the next, smallest to largest. Unlike many large-scale wooden bowl producers, who often make bowls out of pieces of wood and glue them together, Andrew's bowls are hand turned from one piece of wood. His father's design tenets of simplicity and functionality resonate in his work. With a limited range of bowl designs, each offered in a variety of sizes and wood options, he has created a product line with handmade appeal.

Andrew is yet another creative person that Simon and those who he has admired has ultimately shaped. Leach's legacy in teaching potters and craftspeople the skills and values of creating handmade functional objects with beauty was widespread. Philip Pearce's legacy is smaller but he had just as strong an impact on his family. He inspired in his sons, Stephen and Simon, and in his grandson, Andrew, an appreciation of the basic elements of good design combined with a concern for the quality in the materials that each would embrace—clay, glass, and wood—to produce beautiful functional ware of lasting importance.

CHRONOLOGY

Simon's story as a designer and glassmaker can be linked to special individuals and significant events during his youth in Ireland and later in Vermont.

Philip Walter Pearce, a typographer and printer from London, England, and Lucy Helen Crocker, a biologist and university professor, originally from Cardiff, Wales, meet while working in London. They marry in County Cork, Ireland, 1939.

Simon is born in London, England, 1946.

Philip, Lucy, Stephen, Simon, and Sarah Pearce move from London to County Cork, Ireland, 1950.

Philip Pearce and Ivan Allen form a partnership to run the Allen farm in County Cork, Ireland. The Pearce family moves into a wing of Myrtle and Ivan's home, today known as Ballymaloe House.

Philip Pearce decides to pursue a new career as a potter. He purchases Kilmahon House, a former rectory, in the village of Shanagarry, overlooking Ballycotton Bay, and moves his family there, 1954.

Philip Pearce (in a photograph from the late 1950s at work at Shanagarry Pottery) and Lucy Crocker, a university professor and education advocate, were close friends for several years before they decided to marry and start a family.

As a young boy at Cork Grammar School, Simon had difficulties in the classroom. Well over thirty years later, he would discover that he was dyslexic, a learning disability that was little known in Ireland at this time.

Irish Georgian villa architecture, of which Kilmahon House, the Pearce family home for many years, is an excellent example, spread from England to cosmopolitan and rural Ireland. It is exemplified by symmetry, simple proportions, and sophisticated lines.

1960s

Philip Pearce renovates a horse stable at Kilmahon House, 1955. He trains and employs a few local men and women to make pots. Shanagarry Pottery opens for business, 1957. Simon and his brother, Stephen, begin to learn the craft here.

Attends Newtown School, a Quaker boarding school, in Waterford, Ireland, from 1958 to 1962.

An early, small earthenware pitcher by Philip Pearce is in the pottery-making traditions of the region.

Philip Pearce was inspired by the mark that remains on the bottom of a pot when swiped with a piece of wire to relieve it from the potter's wheel and used it as a graphic for his Shanagarry Pottery logo. This mark of authenticity signifies that the pot was thrown on a wheel by hand. Simon later followed his father's example for his own logo, based on the glass pontil mark.

As a teenager, Simon worked in the family pottery, digging and preparing clay, mixing glazes, and packing the kiln. Later, he and his brother, Stephen, learned how to throw pots.

It was at Shanagarry that Simon's apprenticeship would serve as a valuable model for training potters and glassblowers.

At age sixteen, leaves Ireland and travels on a cargo ship to Nelson, New Zealand, to apprentice with English master potter Harry Davis at Crewenna Pottery, 1963.

Embarks on a trip to Japan and the Far East to study indigenous pottery, visiting such potters as Shoji Hamada, 1965–66.

Returns to Shanagarry to work at his father's pottery, 1966.

Sets up his own pottery within Shanagarry Pottery to create his signature pottery designs, 1967.

Captivated by artist Patrick Scott's extensive collection of Georgian glass, Simon decides to learn how to make glassware in the Georgian glassblowing tradition, 1967.

Upon his return from training at Crewenna Pottery, Simon created his own designs in Shanagarry, like this earthenware pitcher.

While he was in Japan, Simon had business cards printed on Japanese rice paper.

An earthenware lidded jar by Simon.

Artist Patrick Scott, a great friend of Philip and Lucy Pearce, was Simon's godfather.

The back door of Scott's Dublin house, leading to the garden. Displayed inside are Scott's many collections, including old glass. He bought a building adjacent to the house and turned it into his studio where Simon was a frequent visitor.

Although unable to meet admission requirements because he never finished high school, Simon was permitted to attend classes at the Royal College of Art in London, 1968. At the time, it was the only school in England that had a Glass Department.

Takes evening glassblowing lessons at Sam Herman's studio, the Glasshouse, in Covent Garden, London, 1968.

Is one of four winners in Córas Tráchtála's 1970 Design Scholarship Scheme, 1970.

Simon made his first glass at the Glasshouse in Covent Garden, London, in 1968.

Designers' awards

The four winners in Coras Trachtala's 1970 Design Scholarship Scheme, with the Minister for Labour and Social Welfare Mr. Brennan. (From left) Michael Whelan, Anne Delap, Sally O'Sullivan and Simon Pearce.

Prestigious scholarships providing funds for young Irish designers to study abroad were established by Kilkenny Design Workshops founder, Córas Tráchtála, and the Irish Export Board. One was awarded to Simon (shown far right), and with one thousand pounds he continued his studies at the Royal College of Art, London, and later at the Gerrit Rietveld Academy, Amsterdam, and at Venini glassworks, in Murano, Italy.

Attends classes at the Gerrit Rietveld Academy, in Amsterdam, 1970.

Takes his first job as an assistant to a master glassmaker Vondelinden, at Leerdam glass factory, in the Netherlands, 1970.

Moves to Murano, Italy, to work as an assistant at Venini glassworks, 1970.

Arrives in Denmark, where he is offered a glassmaking workstation at Kastrup-Holmegaard, 1971.

Visits and trains at Orrefors, Sandvik, and Boda glass factories in Sweden, 1971.

Purchases an old cottage in Bennettsbridge, County Kilkenny, Ireland, and refurbishes it for living. He also builds his first glass workshop, Simon Pearce Glass, on the property, 1971.

Opens a showroom at the workshop, 1972.

Invited by Córas Tráchtála to become a jurist for the 1972 CTT Design Scholarship, 1972.

Invited to become a founding member of the Society of Designers in Ireland, 1972.

Letter asking Simon to support and join the newly formed Society of Designers in Ireland. Since the

1960s, Irish design became an increasingly important national agenda.

The first house Simon renovated was adjacent to the glass workshop he designed and built in the same year.

On the second floor of the glass workshop, Simon created a show-room, where he sold his glass and his father's pottery. From the showroom's balcony, visitors could observe glassblowers in action. This viewing area became a model for his later facilities and workshop stores.

A detail of Simon's first letterhead illustrates his early logo, a line drawing of a gather of glass at the end of a glassmaker's blowpipe, designed by Ruth Gill.

Simon makes the Round wine glass in his first glass workshop in Bennettsbridge.

Opens first retail store, the Glass and Pottery Shop, in Clifden, Connemara, Ireland, 1973.

Opens the Simon Pearce store in Kenmare, Ireland, 1974.

Contributes a magazine article, "Running a Glass Workshop," to *Crafts*, 1976.

Opens the Simon Pearce store in Dublin, 1977.

Designs his first "pontil mark" logo, which appears in Simon Pearce marketing materials, 1976.

Featured in *Hot Glass*, a documentary film by England's National Film School, directed by John Tchalenko, 1977.

When Simon opened a retail store on the fashionable Kildare Street in Dublin, he sold his glassware, his father's pottery, and a few well-chosen items, such as flatware by British industrial designer David Mellor and Danish design company Georg Jensen.

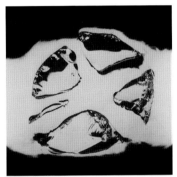

With a felt-tip marker, Simon designed his new logo based on the pontil mark (top), the cross underneath each vessel that is made by the pontil iron, which holds the glass while the rim is hand finished. Through his brochures, he educated customers, stating, "The mark is an integral part of the making process and is consistent with the feeling of the glass as something handmade and personal. For this reason it is left as a distinguishing mark."

The highly successful Round wine glass soon was an icon for Simon Pearce glass, and photographs of it appeared in Simon's marketing materials, as well as in newspaper and magazine articles that featured Simon's story.

1970s

Meets American Patricia (Pia) McDonnell in Ireland, 1977, and they marry in the United States, 1979.

Restores and renovates three old buildings in Bennettsbridge to become his and Pia's new home, 1979.

Pia Pearce takes on sales and marketing and develops the first mail-order catalogue with distribution in Ireland, England, and the United States, 1979.

Simon Pearce glass is advertised in *The New Yorker* magazine, and glass sales exceed expectations.

Simon and Pia McDonnell met in Ireland and were married in Pia's hometown in rural New Jersey. Educated at Stanford University in California and Saint Mary's University of Minnesota, she received a doctoral degree in education at the University of San Francisco. Over the next three decades, she has a crucial role in the company that she and Simon created together.

Just down the lane from Simon's workshop and first house, he bought an old property and revitalized the buildings to become a blend of traditional Irish architecture and contemporary design. It was here that Simon and Pia began a life together and their devotion to design and way of living would continually inform and inspire Simon's glass designs.

Under Simon and Pia's direction and through crisp, clean photography by Kevin Dunne and graphic design by Anton Mazer, the first mail-order catalogue introduces glass for export to a growing audience. The catalogue cover typography was translated into store signage, of which one example still remains on the storefront at the mill in Quechee, Vermont.

1980s

Searches for a new site in North America to establish his glass business and moves to Quechee, Vermont, where the couple renovates an old mill on the Ottauquechee River, 1980.

Irish glassblowers P. J. Skehan, Patrick Kelly, and Charles Shackleton move to Vermont to work with Simon, 1981.

Locates and purchases a turbine from Bridgewater, Nova Scotia, 1981, and installs it at the mill in Quechee, Vermont, 1982.

Simon and Pia move into the mill to live in a renovated loft-style apartment on the second floor, 1981, and start a family: Andrew, born 1981; Adam, born 1984; David, born 1985; and Kevin, born 1987.

The Simon Pearce store opens at the mill, Quechee, Vermont, 1981.

Produces the first catalogue of Simon Pearce glass made in America, 1982.

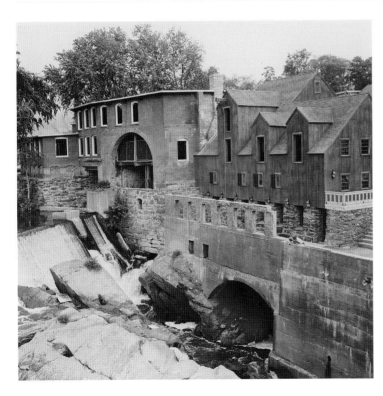

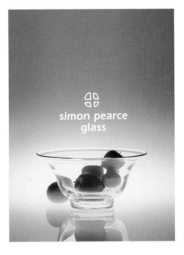

The first building at the mill site dates back to 1807, and by 1813 it consisted of three separate units. The main building was five stories high. In 1869, a flood claimed most of the complex. The following year the mill was rebuilt and substantially renovated over the next century according to the business needs of at least twenty-four owners. When Simon took over the site, it had been the engineering and architectural offices for the

Quechee Lakes Corporation, who maintained office space there until 1983. The most dramatic technical change to the mill in the late twentieth century was the installation of the hydroturbine to harness natural energy from the river to convert it to electricity in order to pay the state power company for the fuel to operate the glass furnaces.

Pia and Simon with their four sons, in a 1994 photograph.

Pia oversaw the first Simon Pearce store in the front lobby of the mill and later expanded the space. She created table settings of Simon's glassware along with pottery by Philip and Stephen Pearce, and imported and sold Irish furniture and crafts—blankets, baskets, table linens, leather goods, and clothing—to create a sense of Simon's Irish heritage.

The first Vermont catalogue introduced Simon Pearce to a new American audience as a designer and blower of handmade glass. It showcased thirty-seven of his glass designs—eleven of which remain in production today—as well as pottery made by his father and brother. The process of making glass and the importance of the pontil mark was pointed out. "It is an absolute guarantee that each piece is handmade, personal, and unique."

Opens the Glassblower's Café at the mill in 1983, and later expands it to become the Simon Pearce Restaurant, with an open-air cantilevered deck for dining, 1986.

An American-born potter who trained in England, Miranda Thomas sets up a pottery at the mill, 1984.

Opens Simon Pearce retail stores in Freeport, Maine; New York City, New York; Charles Square, Cambridge, Massachusetts; Westport, Connecticut; San Francisco, California; Greenwich, Connecticut; Princeton, New Jersey; and Hanover, New Hampshire.

Designs his second version of the "pontil" logo and introduces a new "Simon Pearce" logotype.

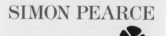

Simon Pearce Glass
The Mill, Quechee
Vermont 05059

(802) 295-2711

SIMON PEARCE

The Simon Pearce Restaurant opened with a menu of traditional Irish and family recipes. A cantilevered open-air dining room with outdoor seating was added, and later was enclosed with glass walls.

In addition to selling his father and brother's pottery, Simon wanted to create a line of his own. Miranda Thomas was instrumental in creating a pottery at the mill and establishing this product category.

When they started their business in the United States, Pia and Simon were mindful of the quantity of designs they produced annually. The quality of their products always came first. Product design went through careful scrutiny and evaluation before anything was released. Simon even took samples of his latest designs for stemware,

bowls, candleholders, and pitchers home to use in his kitchen, a practice he learned from his parents and their pottery.

Simon's hand-drawn logo, which depicted the pontil mark, carried over from Ireland to the United States.

The "Simon Pearce" logotype was eventually composed in ITC Modern #216 Light, a typeface quite similar to the one Simon used for his Dublin store signage. Simon's pontil mark design went through a number of design iterations until it was solidified on a catalogue cover and printed in purple; it remained in that configuration as a brand identity for over twenty years.

Featured in *Gourmet* magazine, 1989.

The pottery moves to Simon's red barn in Hartland, Vermont, and is lost to a fire.

Builds and opens a new glassblowing facility and Simon Pearce store, Windsor, Vermont, 1993.

Hires Swedish-born technical glass engineer Jan Mollmark, 1994.

Builds and opens new pottery facility and warehouse, Windsor, Vermont, 1997.

PLEASURES OF THE TABLE
SIMON PEARCE

BY ZANNE EARLY ZAKROFF

Photographs by Mathias Oppersdorff

Many variables combine to make up what we think of as a perfect meal, and most of them have nothing to do with either food or wine. Convivial company is key under any circumstances, as in a wonderful setting, and in a restaurant situation good service is an important factor as well. But some of the more subtle influences on our enjoyment of a meal, specifically the tableware, are frequently taken for granted. In a desperate situation you know you could drink your wine out of an empty mayonnaise jar instead of from a goblet, but the question is, would you really want to?

From the time you were old enough to claim that kitchen water tasted better than the water from the bathroom tap you've probably had a favorite glass. Then, it may have had a picture of Roy Rogers on it, but it was yours, and above all it made whatever was poured into it taste better. So there you were at age two or three, making an aesthetic judgment, knowing that even a glass of water could be enhanced as much by its vessel as by its origin.

Simon Pearce is a man who knows about such things. It is his passion to make practical items beautiful, enriching the everyday pleasures of food and drink, and he does this near Woodstock, Vermont, at The Mill in Quechee.

The Mill is a unique place to visit, combining as it does a glassblowing operation, an active pottery studio, a retail store, and a serious restaurant. Located on the Ottauquechee river, which provides scenery as well as the power to heat furnaces that melt sand into glass, The Mill would appear to be an excellent contemporary example of Yankee ingenuity. But Simon Pearce is from slightly east of New England, having moved his business to America from Ireland in 1981.

The staggering cost of fossil fuels in Europe was threatening to raise the prices of Simon's glassware beyond reach at about the time the United States government decided to reward, with various incentives, businessmen who were willing to develop alternative energy sources. Recognizing a potentially golden

*Above and right:
Simon Pearce
Restaurant*

56   GOURMET / AUGUST 1989   57

The magazine article about Simon Pearce in *Gourmet* served its readership as a guide to visiting the mill in Quechee. It positioned Simon—his story, glass, and pottery—through the restaurant and its exceptional food, citing the value of making things beautiful at, for, and on the table. At the end of the article, recipes from the restaurant for Ballymaloe brown bread and beef and Guinness stew were included. National awareness of Simon Pearce grew as a result of this highly favorable portrait.

Swedish-born glassmaker Jan Mollmark was residing in England when Simon hired him to work in Vermont. Mollmark's technical and engineering skills allowed glass-making methods to flourish, and he opened up new possibilities for design and production.

English-born potter Jeff Pentland oversaw the growth of the pottery when the new facility opened in Windsor, Vermont.

273

Product development dramatically increases from dozens of product offerings to hundreds.

Shifts from importing Irish-made furniture and soft goods to tabletop home accessories made in Vermont and other parts of the world.

Opens a new glassblowing facility, warehouse, and Simon Pearce store in Mountain Lake Park, Maryland, 1999.

Builds and opens another glassblowing facility, restaurant, and Simon Pearce store on the Brandywine River in West Chester, Pennsylvania, 2000.

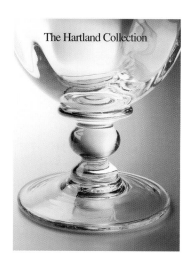

The Hartland Collection

13

Handmade Quality

Simon Pearce has always worked in clear glass. His pieces are all of original design, made with the highest quality craftsmanship and created with two things in mind: beauty and function. The glassblowers work in teams, and each piece is hand blown and hand finished. The rough cross underneath each glass, made by the pontil iron which holds the glass as it is finished, symbolizes the unique nature of each piece. For this reason, the cross is left as the Simon Pearce trademark.

Product lines often expanded to include collections of glassware under the same iconographic design, such as Hartland, noted for its glass ball, which started as a wine glass design and evolved into related designs for bowls, candleholders, and hurricanes.

Table settings continued to be an important feature of the Simon Pearce glass and pottery product catalogues from the 1990s. On the table are Cavendish white wine glasses, Woodbury vases, and Square pottery. Other tabletop items, such as the place mats, napkins, and flatware, came from a variety of sources, and changed frequently to reflect the feeling and colors of the seasons. The table

settings in the catalogues and stores branded the Simon Pearce style. Simon encouraged customers "to buy what you like, what pleases you . . ." suggesting that with his glass, they should make their own creative expressions at home.

Coauthors and publishes *A Way of Living*, with Pia Pearce and Glenn Suokko, 2009.

Receives an honorary Doctor of Humane Letters degree from the University of Vermont, Burlington, in recognition of his contributions to glassblowing and business leadership, 2011.

On August 28 and 29, 2011, Tropical Storm Irene devastates Vermont and the mill is severely flooded, causing considerable damage to it as well as to the covered bridge that provided access to the mill on Quechee's Main Street.

Simon steps back from running the business, although he remains active in providing his ideas and occasional technical and product design support, and Clay Adams is hired as the company's CEO, 2012.

Pia and Simon Pearce and Glenn Suokko collaborated on a project that culminated in the book *A Way of Living*, a creative expression of the couple's way of life and the products of their work: their glass and pottery. Composed of three sections, Simon shares a brief history and his thoughts about glassmaking, and Pia describes the early influences that inspired her to create a hospitable home. Included are favorite recipes from the Simon

Pearce restaurants, which she cooks for her family and friends. The book brought a private life to a devoted audience of Simon Pearce customers. Included are personal stories and interpretations of the Simon Pearce lifestyle.

When Tropical Storm Irene and its subsequent flooding had subsided, the mill had to close for several weeks while reconstruction was underway. It took well over a year to complete the renovations. If there is a silver lining to a catastrophic event, it created an opportunity to improve the old mill. Today, a new glass workshop provides visitors with a welcoming viewing area to see glass made by hand by a talented crew.

After three decades of brand identification, the familiar pontil mark and Simon Pearce logotype are changed in favor of a new brand identity, 2014.

Simon (left) and his older brother, Stephen (right), enjoy a moment together at Stephen's home in Italy, 2015.

ACKNOWLEDGMENTS

Throughout the process of creating this book, I had the support of many individuals to whom I am deeply grateful.

In Vermont, I thank Simon Pearce chief executive officer Clay Adams for his steady commitment to this project, and technical engineer Jan Mollmark for providing his accounts of glass history and of his important collaboration with Simon.

On my research trip to Ireland with Simon in 2015, several individuals offered us not only warm hospitality but also personal perspectives that aided my understanding of his work. In Dublin, I especially acknowledge Margaret Downes for writing about Simon's early days in Ireland and the creativity she encountered at the Pearce's home; and Eric Pierce, who welcomed us into his partner Patrick Scott's house and studio, where we immersed ourselves in Scott's artwork and glass collection. In Shanagarry, Stephen Pearce related many childhood memories of his family life and work at Shanagarry Pottery. In Glengarriff, gallery owner Catherine Hammond opened her home to us and shared her knowledge of art, design, and crafts today.

I am sincerely grateful to Pia Pearce's mother, Peggy McDonnell, and to my extended family, including Pauline Billings and Frank and Hisako Billings, for the opportunities to photograph Simon's glassware in their houses, and to floral designer Carol Magadini, who created several of the arrangements at Pia's mother's house for the lifestyle section. Photographer John Sherman beautifully captured the essence and luminosity of Simon's glass; I thank John for collaborating on many of the stunning images, particularly for "Selected Designs."

In New York, I wish to thank Rizzoli's publisher, Charles Miers, and associate publisher Margaret Rennolds Chace for publishing the first major book on Simon Pearce; senior editor Sandy Gilbert Freidus for her keen insight and organization of this project; and Hilary Ney and Elizabeth Smith for refining my prose.

I thank Pia Pearce for her enduring thoughtfulness and insight, which are greatly treasured. Finally, I wish foremost to thank Simon Pearce for the many interviews and remarkable—often poignant—times we have shared over many years that led to the creation of this book, and for consenting to let me tell his inspiring story.

OPPOSITE
On a desk in my studio, Simon's Revere bowl is a still life container for decorative or found objects, such as a gnarly apple branch.

NOTES

Unless otherwise noted, quoted commentary from Simon Pearce is from author interviews in Quechee, Vermont, August 28, 2013, September 20, 2013, July 8, 2014, and in Shanagarry, Ireland, April 25–May 2, 2015; quoted commentary from Jan Mollmark is from Windsor, Vermont, March 10, 2015.

From Ireland to Vermont: A Life Making Glass

1 Kaj Franck et al. *Design in Ireland: Report of the Scandinavian Design Group in Ireland* (Dublin: Irish Export Board, 1961).

2 Herbert Ypma, *Irish Georgian* (London: Thames & Hudson, 1998), 17.

3 Ibid., 74.

4 *Simon Pearce Glass* (1982), 3.

5 Simon Pearce, *Crafts* (September/October 1976), 31.

6 Terence Conran, "A Note on Good Design," in *Design: Intelligence Made Visible*, by Stephen Bayley and Terence Conran (London: Conran Octopus, 2007), 10–11.

7 Pearce, *Crafts*, 31.

8 Sōetsu Yanagi, *The Unknown Craftsman: A Japanese Insight into Beauty* (New York: Kodansha USA, 2013), 108.

"Good Design": Philip Pearce, Pottery, and the Leach Tradition

1 Michael Cardew, preface to *A Potter's Book*, by Bernard Leach (Great Britain: Transatlantic Arts Inc., 1976), XX.

2 Muriel Rose, *Artist-Potters in England* (London: Faber and Faber, 1955), 13.

3 Harry Davis, *The Potter's Alternative* (repr. New South Wales, Australia: Methuen Australia, 1987).

4 Rose, *Artist-Potters in England*, 12.

5 Ibid., 15.

6 Ibid.

7 Ibid., 22.

8 Emmanuel Cooper, *Lucie Rie: Modernist Potter* (New Haven and London: Yale University Press, 2012), 103.

9 Christopher Benfey, "Michael Cardew: The Potter as Great Modern Artist," *New Republic*, June 3, 2013.

10 Cooper, *Lucie Rie: Modernist Potter*, 116.

11 Bernard Leach, introduction to *The Unknown Craftsman: A Japanese Insight into Beauty*, by Sōetsu Yanagi (New York: Kodansha USA, 1972), 97.

Philip Pearce's black-and-white-glazed Shanagarry plates are the perfect complement to Simon's clear glass and black-handled flatware.

Simon's Nantucket
hurricane, Essex wines,
and Woodbury bowls.

281

BIOGRAPHIES

Simon Pearce and Margaret Downes, Dublin, Ireland, April 2015.

GLENN SUOKKO

Glenn Suokko is an independent book designer and photographer. For over twenty-five years he has designed and produced books for art museums, foundations, and publishers in the United States and Taipei, Taiwan. From 2005 to 2012, he created *Pastoral*, a series of biannual publications that feature profiles on creative individuals and organizations in Vermont. In 2009, he coauthored with Pia and Simon Pearce the book *A Way of Living*. From 2009 to 2013, he was an independent art director, writer, photographer, and creative director for Simon Pearce.

SIMON PEARCE

Foreword writer Simon Pearce started his early creative life as a potter, working in his family's Shanagarry Pottery in County Cork, on the southeastern coast of Ireland. He trained as a glassblower at Glasfabriek Leerdam in the Netherlands, Venini glassworks in Italy, and Orrefors in Sweden. Simon established his glass business in Bennettsbridge, Ireland, in the mid-1970s. He moved to America in 1981, settling in Vermont, to pursue his dream of creating handcrafted utilitarian glass using old-world techniques and the finest raw materials. He and his wife, Pia (McDonnell) Pearce, created Simon Pearce Glass. For nearly forty years, Simon Pearce's glass has been famous for its range of styles, pure materials, and luminosity.

MARGARET DOWNES

Contributing writer Margaret Downes was one of the first women to become a partner in the international professional services firm PricewaterhouseCoopers (PwC) and the only woman to date to be elected president of the Institute of Chartered Accountants in Ireland. She was deputy governor of the Bank of Ireland. Her interest in the visual and performing arts and business acumen led to her to be chair of the Kilkenny Design Workshops, a non-executive director of Terence Conran International design empire, chair of the Emerging Irish Artists Residency competition, and chair of the Dublin International Piano Competition.

Photography

Pia Pearce: page 275 (bottom, far right).

Courtesy Liberties Press, Dublin: page 266 (top right).

Courtesy Simon Pearce: pages 1, 10, 13, 18, 26 (top), 41, 42, 44, 46–47, 49, 52, 61, 230 (top), 249, 256, 262–266, 268–271, and 273–274.

John Sherman: pages 2–3, 7, 38–39, 48 (bottom), 53, 56–60, 64, 126, 129, 131–133, 135, 137, 139, 141–143, 145, 147, 149, 150–171, 173–175, 177, 179, 181, 183–189, 191, 193, 195, 197, 199, 201, 203, 205, 207–209, 211–213, 215, 217, 219, 221–223, 248 (top and middle), and 257.

Glenn Suokko: cover, endpapers, pages 4, 6, 14, 17, 20–24, 26–37, 40, 43, 45, 50–51, 54, 62–63, 65, 66–125, 128, 136, 138, 148, 176, 180, 182, 190, 192, 198, 200, 204, 214, 220, 224–225, 227, 228, 230 (bottom), 232–233, 235–237, 239–247, 248 (bottom), 250–255, 258–261, 267 (left), 275 (left and middle top and bottom), 277, 284, and 286–288.

Excerpted from *The Decorative Arts of Sweden* by Iona Plath, Charles Scribner's Sons, New York and London, 1948: page 48 (top and middle). Collection Glenn Suokko.

FRONT COVER
A collection of Simon's glassware and Philip Pearce's pottery.

PAGE 1
Simon in his first glass workshop in Bennettsbridge, Ireland, early 1970s.

PAGES 2–3
Several of Simon's iconic glass designs.

PAGE 4
A table setting of Simon's glass, pottery, and flatware.

PAGE 6
A Hartland goblet being made at the Simon Pearce glass workshop in Quechee, Vermont.

FOLLOWING SPREAD
The rocky-ledged cliffs along Ballycotton Bay, County Cork, Ireland, May 2015.

PAGE 288
Simon, Ballycotton Bay, County Cork, Ireland, May, 2015.

ENDSHEETS
Detail of a sculpture made from wooden glass molds and tools.

BACK COVER
A collection of Simon's glassware.

First published in the United States of America in 2016 by Rizzoli International Publications, Inc.
300 Park Avenue South
New York, New York 10010
www.rizzoliusa.com

Text copyright ©2016 Glenn Suokko

Photography copyright ©2016 Glenn Suokko (with the exception of photographs listed on left)

2016 2017 2018 2019 / 10 9 8 7 6 5 4 3 2 1

Printed in China

ISBN 13: 978-0-8478-4932-1

Library of Congress Control Number: 2016935613

Project Editor: Sandra Gilbert Freidus

Art Direction and Design: Glenn Suokko

Production: Alyn Evans